101 Companies That Hire Senior Workers

By Arthur Kuman, Jr. and Richard D. Salmon

A Brattle Communications, Inc. Publication

Published by
Brattle Communications, Inc.
24 Computer Drive West
Albany, New York 12205

Cover design by Tim Gresh Associates

Library of Congress Card Catalog Number: 93-074119
ISBN 0-918938-06-6

Manufactured in the United States of America

10 9 8 7 6 5 4 3 2

ACKNOWLEDGEMENTS

We would like to thank the following friends, family and colleagues without whom this book would not have been possible: for assistance in research, Alex Intrator; for assistance in computers and other related matters, Peter Intrator and Ellen Stroope; for cover design, Tim Gresh; for design assistance, Arthur Kuman, Sr.; for accounting information, Ed Feuer; for information regarding the law, Bill Tucker and Joe Simon; for reading and proofing, Janet Nickerson, and Jeannie Clarke for professional input and advice.

And lastly, thanks to Wayne and Tami Colwell, Peg Kuman, and Chris Salmon for their continuing support, help and patience in making this book possible.

Contents

PART TWO

101 Companies That Hire Older Workers

Computers and Electronics

Consumer Products

Financial Services

Health/Pharmaceuticals

Hot Growth

Media/Entertainment

Retail/Mail Order

Transportation/Hospitality

Work At or From Home

Introduction

Golden Age for Mature Workers

The economic news seems to get worse each day. Many of this country's largest employers are laying off more and more workers. Increasingly, these victims of corporate downsizing are white collar, middle managers. Now they're on the street!

Yet even as mid-career individuals are having their exit interviews, America is about to enter a Golden Age for mature workers. Medical science has created a growing, healthier senior population. Older employees are now the fastest growing segment of the workplace, and, the most productive!

Not all companies are cutting jobs!

Many of the companies in this book are actually expanding and creating jobs-full and part-time. They are companies that have made an effort to attract older workers, set up special programs for retraining older employees, arranged special flexible schedules, even actively recruited older workers.

Using This Book

This is the only book of its kind today that is specifically written for people over 50. It's filled with job hints and suggestions, things to keep in mind while you decide what's best for you. Do you want a second career? Can you afford to work part-time? What about doing something on a temporary basis? How about working as a volunteer? There are all sorts of wonderful possibilities for you to choose from!

Selection of Companies

The 101 companies and organizations profiled in this book have a reputation for hiring older workers, or offering specific programs aimed at older workers. They are a diverse group, ranging from giant corporations such as **Wal-Mart** and **UPS** to smaller unheralded gems such as **GardenWay**, **Gallup Organization**, and even the **U.S. Olympic Committee**.

The nominees came from a wide variety of sources. We researched literally thousands of potential companies. A detailed survey was mailed out asking probing questions such as, "What makes you different from other companies in your industry? How do you attract older workers?"

We read annual reports, corporate histories, benefits booklets, newspaper and magazine articles, and talked to many current and former employees.

Companies We Can Learn From

While none of the 101 companies selected should be considered "perfect," they do share one very important characteristic: they all are companies which, because of their policies and programs, attract not just older employees but workers of all ages. These are all companies we can learn from.

All 101 companies exhibit most or all of these 5 characteristics:

- **They are people oriented**
- **They understand the value of older workers**
- **They offer superior pay/benefits**
- **They offer flexible work policies**
- **They offer opportunities such as continuing education and advancement within their organization**

Increased Demand For People Over 50

Every time that a new Wal-Mart is about about to open, the company runs full page recruitment ads in the local newspapers. Part of the advertising copy is an open invitation to older workers, especially retired persons, to come and apply for a position with Wal-Mart.

If you have ever shopped at a Wal-Mart, you will notice that a large number of the sales associates and customer service representatives are older workers. What Wal-Mart already knows and what other smart corporations are learning is that the mature worker is an exceptional choice for many types of work.

Increased demand for older workers is being driven by several factors:

1.The Work Force is Growing Older. There is an increasing number of available older workers and a declining number of "baby boomers." Companies had better keep older workers in mind! According to U.S. government figures, by 2005 workers aged 55 and over will comprise 15% of the labor force, up from 12% in 1990.

2. Companies Need Both Older & Younger Workers. There is a growing appreciation for the stability and reliability of older workers. They have proven themselves. They are the generation we refer to when we speak of "work ethic."

3.Many Companies are Downsizing. The mature worker is frequently looking for precisely those types of jobs that companies are offering today: part-time, seasonal, flexible hours.

8 Good Reasons Why Employers Want Mature Workers

1. Experience. During perilous economic times employers feel there is no substitute for "road time". Experienced older workers can mean increased efficiency and, most of all, large profits.

2. Stability. Older workers are stable.That translates into less employee turnover and greater employee efficiency.

3. Skill. Many times it is the seasoned worker who has the specific skill(s) needed to complete a difficult task.

4. Quality of Work. Older workers have a special appreciation for their jobs. They are trained to produce superior products and services.

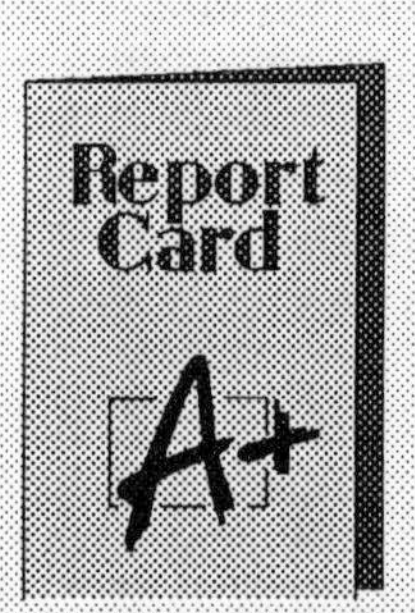

5. Learning Ability. Mature workers can learn just as quickly as younger workers.

6. Productivity. Older workers produce just as much as younger workers and, in many instances, more!

7. Judgment. Good judgment is a by-product of their experience.

8. Reliability. This may be the single greatest asset of mature employees.

What Will You Do With The Rest Of Your Life?

For the worker over 50, still staggering from yet another corporate "restructuring," it seems as though the once orderly world of work has turned into a shambles. Logical career progression no longer seems attainable.

Corporate loyalty, once the hallmark of so many great companies, is just one casualty of the seemingly endless wave of leveraged buyouts. The quest for short term profitability is at the expense of faithful employees.

Yet, a mid-career jolt may turn out to be the best thing that ever happened to you. You may find that it truly is the first day of the rest of your life!

Now is the time to sit down, relax, and think about what you might like to do. Think about the possibilities. Be creative! Do you really want, or need, to work? **Do you have enough money to retire?** (You'll need approximately 80% of your current income to live as comfortably in retirement as you do while working).

Can You Work and Still Collect Social Security?

If you earn too much money working in retirement your social security benefits could be reduced. Does it pay for you to work? To get the answer to that question and others, contact your local Social Security office.

10 ALTERNATIVES TO THE 9 to 5 JOB

Your new job doesn't have to be a 9 to 5 proposition. Here are just 10 alternatives that could very well change your whole outlook on the world of work.

1. Consulting. Someone once said that most consultants were unemployed managers with attaché cases. The fact is that as companies downsize, they are finding it more cost effective to hire consultants for critical tasks.

2. Flextime. This is a way of working which allows you to be in the office for a number of "core" hours, while the rest of your work week is designed around you and your employer's needs. (A good example is starting very early in the day during the summer and leaving the office at 3:00 to enjoy the good weather.)

3. Job Sharing. In this situation a job is designed around more than one person. Each employee is trained to do the other's work, as though they were interchangeable parts.

4. Part-time. Working on a schedule at less than 35 or 40 hours per week may be ideal for those no longer interested in a full time job, but not yet ready to retire.

5. Phased Retirement. Call this a "winding down" period in your career. Phased retirement usually involves reduced hours and abbreviated work weeks.

6. Seasonal Work. Working for a defined period of time may be the best of both worlds for someone who wants to travel or has other commitments during the balance of the year.

7. Starting Your Own Business. This is the secret dream of many people. For mature workers, who have developed expertise, and have accumulated some savings or have access to financial backing, it could be an ideal time to start out on your own. A call to your local Small Business Administration office is one place to get good information.

8. Temporary Help. There are now a number of personnel agencies that specialize in placing older workers as temporaries. Working as a "Temp" gives you an opportunity to observe and be observed. You could eventually get the chance to work on a more permanent basis with a particular firm- if you want to.

9. Volunteer Work. Giving back to your community in the form of volunteer work with non-profit organizations, such as the Red Cross, provides real psychological rewards. It might not make you rich but it could make you some lifelong friends.

10. Work At Home. Tired of commuting? Join the growing number of people who work from their homes. The telephone and computer/FAX have made this a solid alternative to driving to and from work on a regular basis.

The 5 Steps To Getting a Good Job

Attitude

Job hunting is rarely easy, but what differentiates those who are successful from those who are not is quite pure and simple: attitude. Most everyone faces rejection when job hunting, yet it is how you handle that rejection that makes all the difference.

Besides having the right attitude, successful job hunting requires 5 distinct steps:

1. Self-appraisal. The key to finding a good job lies in knowing yourself. What are your qualifications? What motivates you? You need a detailed inventory of your background and experience so you will know what skills and assets you can offer an employer.

2. Develop a game plan. Just as a football team takes great pains to understand what it must do in order to win, you too need to organize your own job search. Set goals! Keep detailed records. What is your timetable going to be? Remember, the number of job offers you receive depends on how well you execute your game plan.

My
Goals

3. Utilize all available resources. You need to develop a list of potential employers. Talk to friends, relatives, and former associates about any job openings they know of. Check your local library to see what they have to offer. Contact employment agencies and trade associations for job leads. Respond to want-ads. Start doing some informational interviewing.

4. Contact potential employers. When you have drawn up a list of employment prospects you will be ready to secure interviews with the persons who have the power to hire you. At this stage, a powerful cover letter, an effective resume, and a knowledge of interviewing techniques, become all important.

GOAL

5. Follow-up. You are not successful until you are on the payroll, and there are several steps you must take after your interview to help you get the job: write a thank you note and follow-up your interview with a phone call several days later.

TIPS FOR A SUCCESSFUL JOB SEARCH

- **Start your search now, not tomorrow. Job hunting is a full-time job!**
- **Set quotas for yourself. Contact a minimum number of people each day.**
- **Be organized. Keep detailed records.**
- **Use any and all resources: friends, former employers, want ads, etc.**
- **Prepare a resume.**
- **Don't be discouraged by set-backs.**
- **Stay flexible. If your strategy is not working, change the strategy!**
- **Look good. Be positive. Smile!**

Shopping For A Job:
9 Strategies That Work

The more strategies you utilize to contact potential employers, the more effective your job search will be. Whether you are interested in something full-time, part-time, or just temporary, here are nine proven strategies:

1. Networking. Not surprisingly, most jobs are filled without ever being advertised. You can tap into this "hidden job market" by asking friends, relatives, and business associates about any job openings they might know of, for referrals, or possibly arranging an introduction with someone who could help.

2. Informational Interviewing. Contact people who are doing the kind of work you would like to do. Find out about the organization's plans and see if you'd like to work there.

3. Professional Trade Associations. It is important to cultivate good relations with fellow members of trade and professional organizations. "Shop talk" is always a good source for job leads.

4. Employment Agencies and Executive Recruiters. Many underplay the value of executive recruiters and employment agencies. Some are excellent. Others are just ineffective. Many, such as Manpower and Olsten, offer many superb part-time and temporary opportunites for older workers.

5. Conventions and Trade Shows. A trade show, professional conference, or annual convention is an ideal setting to make direct contact with prospective employers.

6. Government Agencies. No matter where you go in this country you will find that the government is often the major employer in that area. You will also find that there are individuals working at all levels of the Civil Service who can help you in your job search.

7. Chambers of Commerce. These private organizations are made up of members of the business community. They are among the most important sources of information for any job hunter. Chambers publish many useful brochures and directories with listings of local companies, addresses, and telephone numbers.

8. Want Ads. An ad represents a barometer of a company's fortunes. Regular advertising is a good sign. Pay particular attention to those firms whose ads appear frequently. Even if your qualifications do not quite meet those listed in a particular advertisement, there may be other areas in the company where your talents could be put to use.

9. Other Sources. House organs of many companies list openings for the benefit of current employees. Even an inspection of the directory of tenants usually found in the lobby of large office buildings may turn up names of companies that could be potential employers.

Organizations That Help Older People

There are now associations whose charter is to help older members of the work force. Here are a few good ones that can help you with your job search.

American Association of Retired Persons
601 E Street, N.W.
Washington, DC 20049
(202) 434-2277

AARP is one of the premier organizations for people age 50 and over. While it originally started as an advocacy group for retired people, **AARP** now provides its members with a wide range of services through a nationwide network of local chapters. **AARP WORKS** is an especially good employment planning program for older job hunters that offers first rate publications, materials, and workshops. The best part about **AARP** is that membership costs only $8.00 for one year. You also get ***Modern Maturity*** magazine and the monthly ***Bulletin***.

Here are just a few of the publications you can get free of charge once you become a member of **AARP**:

How to Stay Employable: A Guide for the Midlife and Older Worker

A Winning Resume

Returning to the Job Market: A Woman's Guide to Employment Planning

Catalyst
250 Park Avenue South
New York, NY 10003
(212) 778-8900

Catalyst is a national nonprofit organization that was started over 25 years ago to help women with their careers. It offers many excellent publications as well as counseling services. It also publishes ***Career Development Resources***. Check with its main office in New York City, or your local Yellow Pages, for the office nearest you.

Forty Plus Club of New York, Inc.
15 Park Row
New York, NY 10038
(212) 233-6086

Forty Plus Club is a well known self-help organization designed to assist unemployed people at the professional and managerial level. **Forty Plus Club** offices are staffed entirely by people who are themselves currently out of work. There are chapters in most major cities across America. Check with the main office in New York City or your local Yellow Pages for the office nearest you.

Association of Part-Time Professionals
7700 Leesburg Pike
Suite 216
Falls Church, VA 22043
(703) 734-7975

A national nonprofit organization that offers information on flexible work arrangements.

7 WAYS TO COMPETE WITH YOUNGER WORKERS

1. Emphasize your experience. Don't ever mention or apologize for your age. It is unimportant!

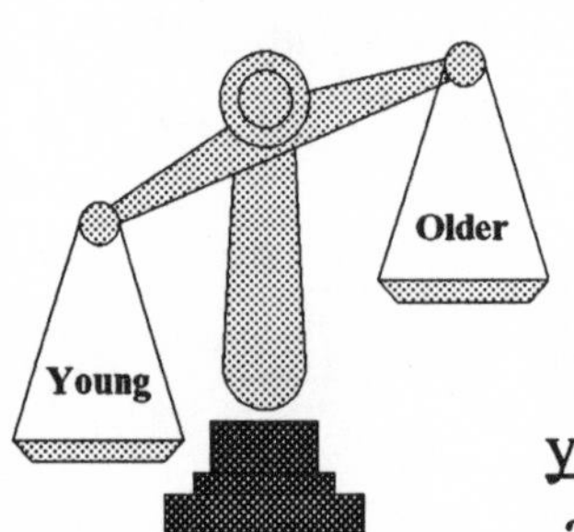

Emphasize what skills and experience you do have; what you can do for an organization.

Your experience actually gives you a competitive edge over younger workers. Use that advantage!

2. Stay healthy. Look good! Exercise regularly. Stay fit and trim. The healthier you look the faster people forget about your age.

3. Develop a contemporary image. First impressions are important, no matter what your age. Be careful about the clothes you select for your interview. Hairstyle and good grooming are also important.

4. Watch your language. Your speech should be as up to date as your clothes. Stay away from topics and expressions that clearly date you. Most important of all: DO NOT EXHIBIT PREJUDICES.

5. Stay educated. Keep abreast of news and trends in your occupational field. Learn new things! Improve your skills. Take a computer class. <u>You be the one people look to for answers!</u>

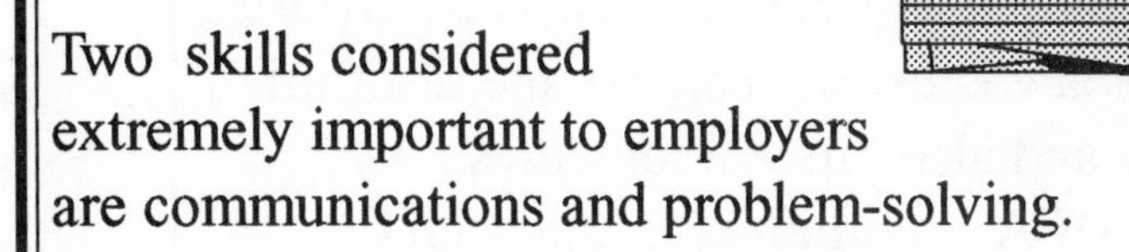

Two skills considered extremely important to employers are communications and problem-solving.

6. Continue networking.
This should be a lifelong process. The majority of new jobs are gotten through a network of professional and social contacts. Stay in touch!

7. No grandchildren, please. A job interview is no time to talk about your grandchildren. Leave the bragging and pictures at home until the job is yours.

Age Discrimination in Employment Act

Discrimination in the work place based on age is one of the nastier realities of life. As a result, in 1967 the United States Congress passed the Age Discrimination in Employment Act (ADEA). The purpose of this law is to help combat age discrimination and also provide remedies for it. The ADEA is administered through the nationwide offices of the Equal Employment Office Commission.

The way for the mature worker to begin to deal with the possibility of age discrimination is to be armed with the facts. The AARP has produced a 20 page booklet entitled **Age Discrimination** on the Job that is worth reading cover to cover. It is an excellent primer on the subject. At the end of the book is a complete listing of all of the EEOC offices located throughout the U.S., including their telephone numbers. Contact your local EEOC office if you suspect age discrimination on the job!

Tips For Writing A Good Cover Letter

"This is NO time to be modest!"

What is a cover letter?

A cover letter is your personal introduction to potential employers. It shows how your experiences and skills match those of a specific position.

Contents:

1. **Opening paragraph.** Explain how you heard about the position and why your background would be an asset.

2. **Middle paragraph(s).** Summarize highlights of your experience that relate to the position you are applying for.

3. **Closing paragraph.** Ask for an interview. Say you will call in a few days to arrange a date and time.

COVER LETTER TIPS

- **A cover letter should accompany every resume you submit.**
- **Always use a typed original.**
- **Always direct your letter to a specific individual.**
- **Sound confident! Make the reader eager to see you.**
- **Be brief and to the point. State the position or area you are interested in and how your skills will help the employer.**
- **Vary cover letters to suit needs of each individual company.**
- **Mention accompanying resume.**
- **Use 8 1/2" x 11" quality paper.**
- **Proofread for errors.**

A Winning Resume

What is a good resume?

A good, effective, resume is an advertisement of yourself designed to communicate your qualifications to potential employers. It is a summary, in outline form, of who you are, what you have done, and your future capabilities.

Whole books are devoted to the subject of resume preparation. Check out several different ones at your local bookstore or library and chose a resume format which presents your job history most favorably.

RESUME TIPS FOR OLDER WORKERS

- **Your resume should not be cast in stone! Keep it up to date and vary it to suit the needs of each particular job.**
- **Be factual. NEVER lie. Concentrate on your strengths. Do not exaggerate to excess, but sell yourself.**
- **Make sure your resume is visually appealing, well organized, and easy to read. De-emphasize dates and years.**
- **Keep sentences and paragraphs short. Use indented and bulleted statements and lots of action verbs.**
- **Use percentages and dollar amounts to specify your impact on an organization.**
- **Omit personal information such as age, height, weight, marital status. Do not use "I," salary information, or pictures.**
- **Resume should be printed on 8 1/2" x 11" quality stock. One page is standard, two are acceptable.**
- **Proofread for errors.**

Effective Interviewing

"Prepare better than your competitors!"

How to Prepare

Common sense should guide your interviewing techniques. Here are some specific recommendations regarding all interviews:

1. Do your homework. Research the company, the job, and the person you will work for. Your knowledge is a measure of your interest in working there. If there is an annual report available, get a copy and study it before the interveiw.

2. Practice your interviewing skills. Role play if necessary. Think about questions you might be aked and how you would respond.

3. Look and feel your best. This means being well rested, dressing appropriately, and maintaining a positive frame of mind

4. Be prompt for the interview. Get directions if necessary. Always leave time for the unexpected.

5. Take an active part! Ask questions. Be enthusiastic, confident, and interested.

6. Salary negotiations. These should be left until the end of an interview or until a second or even third interview. Be honest about your present salary.

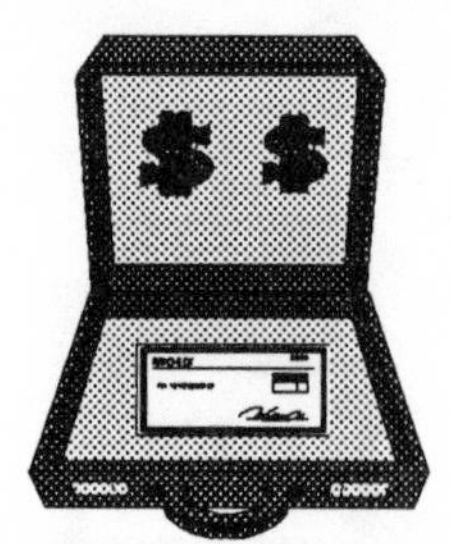

7. Find out. When will the company most likely make a decision? Thank the interviewer for his or her time.

FAVORITE INTERVIEW QUESTIONS

Why do want to work here?

Why do you want to be in this business?

Are you looking for a permanent or temporary job?

Have you done the best work you are capable of doing?

What are your qualifications?

How would you describe yourself?

What is your greatest strength?

How do you interact with people at different levels?

What kind of salary are you expecting?

How long will you stay with the company?

What other companies have you applied to?

101 Companies That Hire Senior Workers

Computers and Electronics

EMPLOYMENT OUTLOOK

The computer and electronics industry will continue to experience industrywide consolidation (through mergers and buy-outs) as large companies like Apple and DEC, and newer companies like AST Research and Dell, fight for market-share, while trying to keep expenses under tight control.

Growth areas will be software development, parts assembly, systems integration, workstations, laptops, and services.

JOBS IN DEMAND

Tens of thousands of new jobs will be created in the computer and electronics industry over the next decade as the market shifts more toward software and computer services. Look for overseas markets to increase in importance as the U.S. market continues to be less profitable.

Best bets: computer systems analysts, programmers, engineers, development managers, marketers, parts assemblers, and sales reps.

APPLE COMPUTER, INC.

20525 Mariani Avenue
Cupertino, CA 95014
(408) 996-1010

Apple's Team Management Style

Like other high tech companies, getting a job at Apple is not easy, especially with recent restructuring and other cost cuts to restore growth.

Yet Apple truly is a one-of-a-kind company. Employees are encouraged to work with all levels of management, to share ideas, and to support each other in a very open atmosphere.

Be organized! Keep records of names, dates, companies, telephone calls, etc.

Apple wants **innovators**, people who'll give them an edge over the competition, people capable of creating ingenious electronic devices such as the popular Powerbook, or the Newton Message Pad, the most advanced of a new group of products known as PDAs, or "personal digital assistants." The Newton is different from anything Apple has done before and offers a great deal of promise, possibilities, and profits.

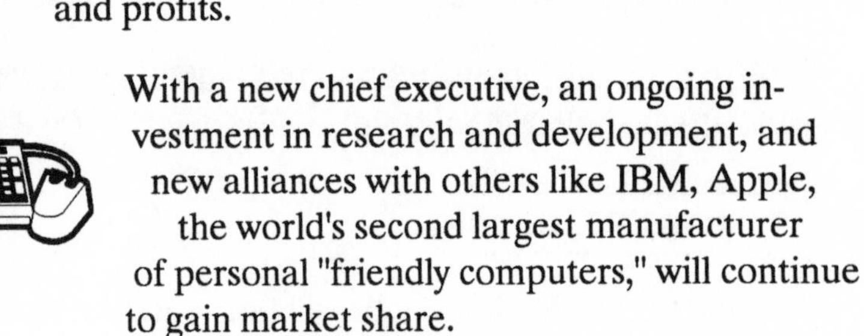

With a new chief executive, an ongoing investment in research and development, and new alliances with others like IBM, Apple, the world's second largest manufacturer of personal "friendly computers," will continue to gain market share.

• •

AST RESEARCH, INC.

16215 Alton Parkway
Irvine, CA 92713
(714) 727-4141

By developing high performance personal computers quickly, and selling them at attractive prices, AST has become one of America's hottest computer companies!

AST Computers Are Built In-House!

Unlike many others in the computer industry, AST designs, manufactures, and assembles all of its products in-house. No wonder it delivered its one-millionth computer just four short years after entering the highly competitive computer systems business!

Just recently AST acquired Tandy's personal computer business, now making it the fifth largest PC manufacturer in the U.S.

Through even faster product development, more efficient manufacturing, and aggressive marketing both here and abroad of its cost-effective computers, AST shall continue to be a good source of jobs. Best bet: marketing, R & D, customer service and support.

• •

DELL COMPUTER

9505 Arboretum Boulevard
Austin, TX 78759
(512) 338-4400

Dell Computer continues to increase its market share by selling high performance IBM compatible PCs, primarily by means of its well trained telemarketing personnel and a national sales force.

Service, Service, Service

Dell's success has been achieved through "**value pricing,**" a package of features that includes: low prices, customer configuration of computer systems to specific customer orders, technical support direct from the manufacturer, and outstanding service.

Utilize any and all resources: friends, former employers, want ads, etc.

Dell continues to add full and part-time employees as it redesigns its computers to meet more sharply defined market niches, and focuses more on profits and cost-cutting.

DIGITAL EQUIPMENT CORPORATION

146 Main Street
Maynard, MA 01754
(508) 493-5111

As one of the world's largest manufacturers of networked computer systems and associated peripheral equipment, Digital is no longer trying to do everything for everybody. With a new president and chief executive, Digital is revamping products and concentrating its efforts on computer networking, software, storage, semiconductors, and services.

Comprehensive benefits and training

Digital "wants and needs new talent!" Employees receive a comprehensive benefits package and are offered extensive training programs at company facilities.

Current areas of need at Digital include: sales, product development and marketing, field support, and manufacturing. Digital is also known for aggressively seeking out qualified female and minority employees.

• •

GENERAL ELECTRIC

3135 Easton Turnpike
Fairfield, CT 06431
(203) 373-2211

With roots that go all the way back to Thomas Edison's 1879 invention of the incandescent lightbulb, GE has become one of the world's most diversified business enterprises, offering an exceptionally broad range of job opportunities for people of all ages.

The company's 12 businesses include everything from high tech manufacturing to all kinds of business services.

Best managed company

"GE is one of the best managed companies in America!" boasts Alex Intrator, a retired GE executive. "They have exceptional resources and enormous technical breadth. And unlike most other companies they give their employees **flexibility**."

GE offers comprehensive benefits and excellent pay. They are famous for their training and improvement classes, and they have an excellent record for hiring women and minorities.

• •

HEWLETT-PACKARD COMPANY

3000 Hanover Street
Palo Alto, CA 94304
(415) 857-1501

"Best Company" lists continually include this big computer maker, and for good reason. H-P is a company characterized by an open atmosphere, where things like teamwork and flexibility are emphasized.

Despite the fact that this multi-billion dollar electronics giant offers more than 10,000 products and systems (including 70%of the market for laser-jet PC printers), it has not forgotten that its greatest asset is the 100,000 people it employs worldwide.

H-P offers superior pay and benefits packages, flextime scheduling, profit sharing, continuing education programs, elder-care resource and referral services, dependent care leaves, part-time opportunities, and even short-time job guarantees. Plus, H-P has many telecommuters.

Currently looking for: Computer education instructors/consultants.

MICROSOFT CORPORATION

One Microsoft Way
Redmond, WA 98052
(206) 882-8080

At Microsoft, the biggest maker of PC operating systems and PC software in the world, people work hard and play hard. The work hours can be long, 60-80 hours per week, but the lucrative stock options can make it easier to take.

In fact, a large percentage of employees at Microsoft have become millionaires, at least on paper. (Nearly all software developers receive stock options when hired.)

Microsoft aims to expand from software for independent computers to work-group computing and is looking to invent an operating system for future televisions.

People With Commitment

In a recent **Business Week** article, William Gates said that what makes successful workers are "Smart people, people with high energy levels, people with commitment to persevere through inevitable dismal periods and see beyond them."

Best bets for jobs: product development, software engineers, software test engineers, and positions within consulting services.

• •

PITNEY-BOWES, INC.

One Elmcroft Road
Stamford, CT 06926
(203) 356-5000

Based in Stamford, Connecticut, Pitney-Bowes is the world's largest manufacturer of postage meters and mailing equipment. This "multinational manufacturing and marketing" corporation also supplies copiers, dictaphones, facsimile systems, tracking systems, business supplies and services, and product financing.

No Compulsory Retirement Age

Profit and innovative products at Pitney-Bowes come as a result of having happy, talented, productive employees. This is a place where people are treated fairly, where employees pool their talents and work together in self-directed teams.

There are always opportunities to try new things at Pitney-Bowes, to take on new responsibilities. Benefits are very good, there is no compulsory retirement age, and employees have many flexible work options.

Best bets for jobs: research and development, office services, and management.

• •

TANDY CORPORATION

1800 One Tandy Center
Fort Worth, TX 76102
(817) 390-3700

As the largest retailer of consumer electronics in the world, Tandy has over 7,000 Radio Shack stores throughout the U.S. and Mexico.

In order to meet the needs of a changing marketplace, Tandy has decided to "spin off" its manufacturing operation into a new company, TE Electronics, Inc. It will also expand the company's Incredible Universe, a chain of giant electronics superstores, and its Computer City stores.

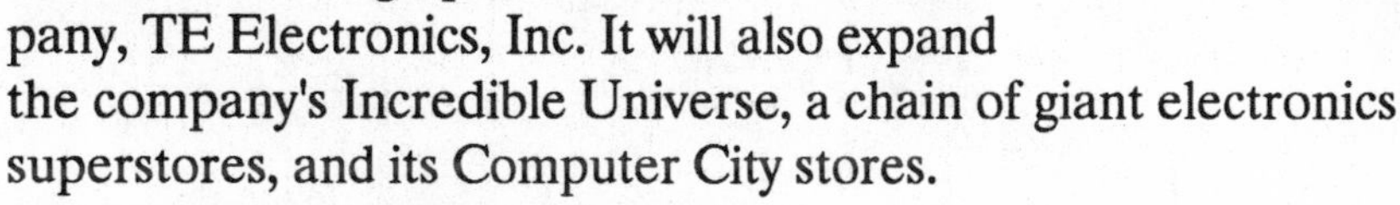

New Markets Mean New Jobs

This restructuring will allow Tandy to develop many new products, sell to other retailers, and open up many new stores in highly populated areas that do not currently have large Radio Shack stores.

Consumer Products

EMPLOYMENT OUTLOOK

Consumer products companies will continue fighting to grab market share from competitors in order to improve their current profit margins. Consolidation, merging with or acquiring other companies in order to quickly add new products and increase market share, shall continue industry-wide.

Companies will continue investing heavily in new products, expanding current brands lines, and pushing toward more and more international sales. Look for huge growth in wireless communication!

JOBS IN DEMAND

Best bets: research & development, product managers, marketers, salespeople, purchasing, and people with broad international experience.

• •

AMOCO

200 East Randolph Drive
Chicago, IL 60601
(312) 856-6111

Encouraging "entrepreneurial" spirit

It might seem unusual to suggest good employment prospects at Amoco. After all, this leader of the Big Oil fraternity has recently restructured, laying off several thousand employees. (Similar downsizing has taken place at Chevron, Atlantic Richfield, and Texaco.) Yet even as this restructuring is occurring, AMOCO has been implementing a stock-option program to encourage a more entrepreneurial spirit among its staff.

Companies want "seasoned" job applicants

Experienced Engineers Wanted!

AMOCO has selected 20 areas throughout the world as high potential locations for oil and gas exploration. As foreign drilling progresses, AMOCO will require the services of mature, experienced petroleum engineers.

In the retail market, AMOCO is expanding the number of service stations it maintains. As a sign of the times, AMOCO is also starting to sell compressed natural gas for use as a motor vehicle fuel. This will increase the need for service station attendants. Finally, for people living in the Chicago area, AMOCO remains a source for accounting and petroleum marketing positions.

AT&T

32 Avenue of the Americas
New York, NY 10013
(212) 841-4666

As the largest U.S. telecommunications company, AT&T has gone back to the kind of aggressiveness that came after Alexander Graham Bell first shouted into a telephone, "Mr. Watson. Come here. I want you."

AT&T, McCaw Deal

By agreeing to merge with McCaw Cellular, the USA's largest cellular-phone network, AT&T has jumped right into a huge growth area: **wireless communications.** AT&T may well combine long-distance services with local cellular services, and possibly even create a cellular network (bypassing the regional Bells). Telecommunications will soon revolutionize the way we live.

Progressive Company

AT&T has always enjoyed a reputation as a progressive company, providing such benefits as elder-care counseling and new skills training for workers whose factories were closing. AT&T's salaries are among the best in the industry. It offers flexible working hours and even work-at-home opportunities.

Women and Minorities

AT& T is also one of only a few businesses that has altered its layoff policy to keep recently hired women and minorities.

● ●

ADOLPH COORS COMPANY

Golden, CO 80401
(303) 279-6565

The Adolph Coors Company is one of those great American corporations around whose principal product, Coors Beer, there has grown a devoted following. For a long time Coors was bottled and distributed only in the Rocky Mountain West. Now, all of that's changed, and the legendary "Water of the West " is found throughout the entire U.S.

Key Source Of Jobs

With nearly 15, 000 employees, Coors has always been regarded as a stable employer and one of the key sources of jobs in the Denver region. A recent decision to "spin off" its non-brewing product lines will allow the nation's 3rd largest brewer to focus even more carefully on its core business.

Don't apologize for your age!

Look for most employment opportunities to be within the Greater Denver region in areas such as product innovation, marketing and production as Coors works aggressively to gain market share under the first non-family president in the history of the Coors Brewing Company.

• •

CORNING, INC.

Houghton Park
Corning, NY 14831
(607) 974-9000

Thousands of Products

While most people still associate Corning with glass (in 1989 Corning formally changed its name from Corning Glass to Corning, Inc.), this New York State based firm now manufactures some 60,000 products!

Corning now competes in such fields as optical fibers, lab services, and specialist materials. Its chain of clinic testing labs, **Metpath, Inc.** has been especially successful, now employing nearly 30,000 full and part-time people nationwide.

Happy & Involved Employees

Corning firmly believes that happy employees can only mean better products, bigger profits, and less turn over. Workers are involved in all facets of operations, voicing their opinions, and helping to maintain quality. Benefits are excellent and all employees get a corporate performance bonus based on the company's profits.

Corning encourages job-sharing, offering options for part-time and work-from-home opportunities, and requires all its people to spend 5% of their work time each year in training.

• •

DIALAMERICA MARKETING, INC.

960 MacArthur Boulevard
Mahwah, NJ 07495
(201) 327-5400

The growth of modern telemarketing during the past decade has created thousands of full and part-time job opportunites.

With over 60 branch offices nationwide, DialAmerica is one of the oldest and largest telemarketing firms in the U.S.

Flexible People Wanted Of All Ages!

DialAmerica is a "full-service" telemarketing agency offering computer supported outgoing services. Its success is due in large part to its diverse workforce. The company is constantly on the lookout for articulate, flexible people of all ages. They hire part-timers and their trained reps are paid a very good hourly base pay to which are added a number of incentives.

Emphasize your skills and experience.

With growth projections for the telemarketing industry looking very impressive (thanks to the explosion of such things as infomercials and 900 numbers), DialAmerica is a company well worth considering.

DU PONT

1007 Market Street
Wilmington, DE 19898
(302) 774-1000

Based in Wilmington, Delaware, Du Pont is the largest chemical company in the U.S., and has been in business for nearly 200 years. For many years Du Pont has been ranked as one of the top companies in FORTUNE magazine's Annual Corporate Reputation Survey.

Du Pont conducts operations in 40 different countries and within 5 diverse business segments:

- o **Chemicals** (commodity and specialty products)
- o **Fibers** (Nylon, Dacron, Lycra, etc.)
- o **Polymers** (such as Teflon)
- o **Petroleum** operations (Conoco)
- o **Diversified** businesses (agriculture, coal, electronics)

Building Employee Loyalty

Du Pont has found that offering such things as flexible scheduling, job sharing, compressed work week, and other alternatives to the typical 9 to 5 job weeks helps build employee loyalty. "I couldn't find this kind of flexibility elsewhere!" says one of their employees.

• •

GARDEN WAY, INC.

102nd Street & 9th Avenue
Troy, NY 12180
(518) 235-6010

Garden Way is known nationwide as the manufacturer of high quality reliable outdoor power equipment such as its famous Troy-Bilt Roto Tiller as well as Bolens tractors and mowers.

Garden Way has long had a reputation as a good place to work.

The work environment is friendly, pay and benefits very good, and work options excellent. The opportunities for advancement are especially good. It is not uncommon for someone to start working on an assembly line or as a copy person and be promoted to any number of other positions.

Seasonal hiring

Most of the hiring at Garden Way is done for Spring and Fall peaks, but do not let that stop you from applying to this exceptional manufacturing company.

• •

GENERAL MILLS

One General Mills Boulevard
Minneapolis, MN 55440
(612) 540-2311

General Mills is a marketing driven firm that very much believes in giving people HANDS-ON TRAINING. The company is constantly looking for talented sales and advertising people, and is especially good at hiring women and minorities.

While most other foodmakers have struggled through the current recession, this Minneapolis conglomerate continues to earn impressive profits thanks to popular foods such as Cheerios, Wheaties, Betty Crocker cake mixes, and Pop Secret popcorn.

Fastest Growing Segment

More than 75% of General Mills employees work in the company's restaurant division, its fastest growing segment. The Red Lobster and Olive Garden chains, with nearly 1,000 restaurants, are highly successful and offer excellent employment options, as well as superb benefits programs.

H & R BLOCK, INC.

4410 Main Street
Kansas City, MO 64111
(816) 753-6900

10,000 Offices Worldwide

Based in Kansas City, Missouri, H & R Block is the world's largest tax preparation firm. It currently operates more than 10,000 offices worldwide, and prepares more than 15 million individual, partnership, and corporate tax returns each year.

Get interviews with people you want to work for!

Many H & R Block offices operate as franchises, hiring an average of 2 full-time and 2 part-time employees. Prior industry experience is helpful but not mandatory. Training is provided and many offices hire seasonal help during peak tax season.

Best bets: Income tax preparer, management trainee, branch manager, bookkeeper.

• •

JOHNSON & JOHNSON

One Johnson & Johnson Plaza
New Brusnwick, NJ 08933
(908) 524-0400

Employees at Johnson & Johnson are made to feel as if they're part of a family. They don't want to leave. People are well paid, they're given many opportunities for development and advancement, and they are eligible for flexible work schedules.

One reason for Johnson & Johnson's impressive record of success (it has never posted a loss) is that unlike most other corporations, Johnson & Johnson is able to enter new markets quickly and produce new products quickly. It is a highly decentralized family of 166 "units." Each unit or division is run like an autonomous company, each has its own management board and each does its own planning and hiring.

It's no wonder then that when FORTUNE magazine recently did a survey of the country's most admired corporations, Johnson & Johnson was ranked near the top.

Current Areas of Need: Johnson & Johnson's health care domination will require a steady supply of sales representatives, marketing analysts, chemists and accountants to serve in the consumer products, professional products, and pharmaceuticals divisions.

• •

LEVI STRAUSS ASSOCIATES, INC.

1155 Battery Street
San Francisco, CA 94111
(415) 544-6000

Levi Strauss never imagined that the rugged French cotton he used to make clothes for Gold Rush miners would eventually become the modern jean, worn by millions throughout the world.

Today, this San Francisco based blue jean maker is now a five billion dollar corporation employing over 30,000 people throughout the U.S.

Levi has long recognized the importance of providing a caring work atmosphere. They were one of the early corporations to introduce job sharing. Their benefits are excellent. (In fact, a recent magazine ranked Levi #1 among all companies for employee benefits.)

At company headquarters there are numerous opportunities for flexible scheduling, work-from-home (upon supervisor approval), compressed work weeks, and part-time positions..

• •

MCI COMMUNICATIONS CORPORATION

1133 19th Street, NW
Washington, DC 20036
(202) 872-1600

MCI is the 2nd largest long distance telephone company in the U.S., providing services to millions of residential customers, businesses, Federal and state governments, and other organizations.

Keep your skills up to date.

Known for innovative work programs, flexible work policies, comprehensive benefits packages, and competitive salaries, MCI is constantly looking to provide its customers with better products and services. It is also not afraid to go outside the company to hire good people.

Wireless Communications

MCI's recent alliance with British Telecommunications gives the company great resources for growth. MCI could very well buy a nationwide wireless phone system (to compete with No.1 AT&T.)

• •

HERMAN MILLER, INC.

8500 Byron Road
Zeeland, MI 49464
(616) 772-3300

Based in Western Michigan, Herman Miller is an office furniture maker with nearly 6,000 employees.

It is a company that believes profit is important, but so is the welfare of each and every employee.

All Employees Are Stockholders

Worker participation has always been paramount at Herman Miller. Employees work in teams in order to give everyone more freedom to accomplish tasks, and also to cut down on the red tape so common at many other companies.

A job well done means good things for everyone since all Herman Miller employees are stockholders in the company.

Herman Miller is a company filled with happy workers. With a new CEO on board, the company looks to continue its tradition of growth, opportunity, and generous employee benefits.

• •

3M

3M Center
St. Paul, MN 55144
(612) 733-1110

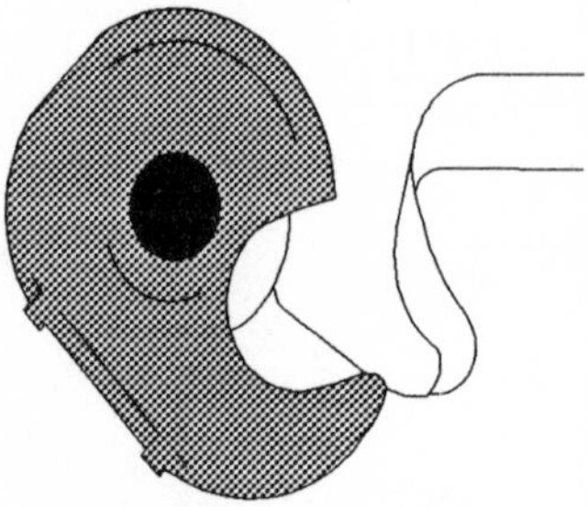

Where It Is Hard To Get Hired

3M (Minnesota, Mining, and Manufacturing) is one place it is hard to get hired. Competition is fierce. People here are "career employees." Few leave, and the company is very big at promoting from within.

Should you be lucky enough to be hired, opportunites abound. Founded in 1902, 3M is extremely diverse. It manufactures and markets more than 60,000 products: consumer and industrial products, surgical dressings, pharmaceuticals, surveillance devices, adhesives, pressure sensitive tapes, traffic control systems, and other highly specialized products.

3M employees are even rewarded for coming up with new ways to use old products.

What 3M Is Looking For

3M doesn't hire "resumes." It hires people. The company wants team players, people who are willing to learn, people who can share and have fun at the same time. "Increased responsibility is assigned commensurate with experience and job performance."

• •

PEPSICO, INC.

700 Anderson Hill Road
Purchase, NY 10577
(914) 253-2000

One of the most admired corporations in the world, Pepsico has a reputation for hiring, training, and keeping its employees happy and challenged. Pepsico's promotion of women and minorities has especailly received a lot of press.

Largest Restaurant System In The World

Pepsico operates within 3 different market areas: soft drinks, market foods, and fast-food restaurants.

Pepsico manufactures and sells such well-known soft drinks as Pepsi, Slice, and Mountain Dew. Its restaurant division-the largest total restaurant system in the world-consists of Pizza Hut, Taco Bell, and KFC. Pepsico's snack division manufactures such well-known brands as Fritos, Lay's, and Doritos.

Pepsico pays well, offers very good benefits, and continues to grow through smart acquisitions, thus offering a wide variety of full and part-time jobs opportunities.

SHERWIN-WILLIAMS COMPANY

101 Prospect Avenue, NW
Cleveland, OH 44115
(216) 566-2000

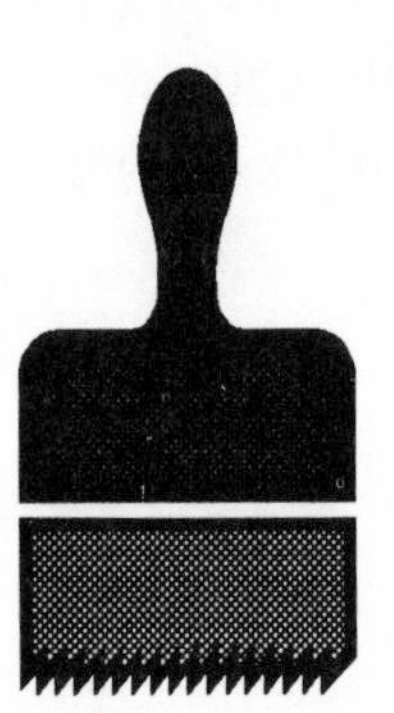

Largest Paint Maker In The World

Cleveland based Sherwin-Williams is the largest paint manufacturer and distributor in the world.

It sells such popular coatings as Dutch Boy, Kem-Tone, plus numerous private label brands to independent dealers, major chains, and home improvement centers.

With nearly 2,000 company owned specialty paint and wallcovering stores in 48 states, Sherwin-Williams continues to seek people for management, sales, and marketing positions at locations throughout the country. Sherwin-Williams offers formal training for highly motivated individuals, as well as a comprehensive benefits package and many flexible work options.

• •

SOUTHWESTERN BELL CORPORATION

One Bell Center
St. Louis, MO 63101
(314) 235-9800

Headquartered in St. Louis, SW Bell is a "family of growing companies offering communication services and products to customers in regional, national, and international markets". It's principal subsidiaries include:

One of the largest cellular telephone operations in the U.S.
The nation's largest paging company (Metromedia Paging Services)
Directory advertising (Southwestern Bell Yellow Pages)
Full-service printing operation (Gulf Printing)

Benefits are first rate and there is an abundance of job training programs for employees to take advantage of.

SW Bell and its subsidiaries offer a wide variety of job opportunities: management positions in engineering, information services, sales, accounting, marketing, communications, finance, and planning. This Bell is moving aggressively into cable TV as well as into the area of "personal communications systems".

• •

THE STANLEY WORKS

1000 Stanley Drive
New Britain, CT 06053
(203) 225-5111

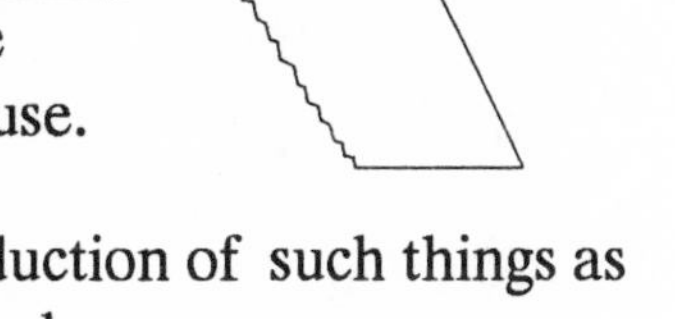

Through effective "teamwork," Stanley has become the largest producer of high quality hand tools in the world for consumer home improvement, industrial, and professional use.

Stanley is also a major factor in the production of such things as hinges, fasteners, air tools, and hydraulic tools.

Worker Directed Facilities

"Several of Stanley's businesses have worker-directed facilities." They include a number of plants where people are empowered to participate in running the operations. (This helps keep product quality high and order turnaround very fast.)

Stanley is very supportive of education and training to upgrade its people. Employees can receive instruction in everything from communication to "just-in-time manufacturing". Best of all: the pay of employees increases with each new skill!

As economic conditions continue to improve, Stanley's operations are poised for growth, offering all sorts of unique employment opportunities.

● ●

STEELCASE, INC.

Box 1967
Grand Rapids, MI 49501
(616) 247-2710

Headquartered in Grand Rapids, MI, Steelcase is the largest designer and manufacturer of office furniture and furniture systems in the world. "Excellence" is a word that has become synonymous with Steelcase products.

Supportive Employee Policies

Steelcase is a family-oriented company, widely recognized for its supportive employee policies and profit sharing bonuses. These are two reasons why, despite the fact that there are over 18,000 employees, the company has such a low turn over rate.

Excellent Wages & Work Options

Pay and benefits are first-rate and most workers have options such as job sharing, flexible, and part-time work opportunities.

Typical job openings: Product development, manufacturing, engineering, industrial design, research and development, and computer systems.

US WEST, INC.

7800 East Orchard Road
Englewood, CO 80111
(303) 793-6500

Formed by the breakup of AT&T in 1984, US West now has telephone operations in 14 western and midwestern states. It currently provides telephone service to over 25 million residential and business customers.

While this communications giant continues to modernize its phone network (thus allowing transmission of video and huge amounts of data), it remains sensitive to the needs and wants of its employees. US West is widely recognized for its employee support groups, self-managed work teams, skills upgrading, and workshops.

Lots Of Telecommuters

US West encourages all sorts of flexible work arrangements: flextime, job sharing, flexible scheduling, part-time work, and compressed work weeks. They are also extremely supportive of "telecommuting."

A good interview can earn you a good job.

As US West continues to expand into European countries and the former Soviet Union and develops partnerships with cable companies outside its region, the overall job outlook remains excellent.

WM. WRIGLEY JR. COMPANY

410 North Michigan Avenue
Chicago, IL 60611
(312) 644-2121

Wm. Wrigley Jr. Company is the largest producer of chewing gum in the world. Wrigley brands are manufactured in 12 factories around the globe and sold in 100 countries. Popular brands include Wrigley's Doublemint and Juicy Fruit.

Amurol Products, Wrigley's fast growing subsidiary, produces such well known products as Hubba Bubba bubble gum, Big League Chew, and Reed's Candy.

Very Good Benefits Package

Long known as a fiscally conservative company, Wrigley continues to hold down long term debt, increase market share, and add new employees. It offers a variety of job opportunities, a very good benefits package, career planning, and flexible work schedules.

Financial Services

EMPLOYMENT OUTLOOK

The long term outlook looks good for insurance companies as they target the needs of our aging population, cope with new regulations (such as a possible government health plan), and offer "new and improved financial services." Competition will remain fierce as companies seek to attract new customers while holding on to old ones.

Employment is expected to increase only slightly within the banking industry. Bank mergers will continue to help increase market share and raise capital. The relaxation of a number of banking regulations should allow banks to better compete with insurance companies, major corporations, and other financial services firms.

JOBS IN DEMAND

Best bets: retirement and financial planners, insurance agents, mutual fund sales, new product development, experienced marketers.

AETNA LIFE & CASUALTY COMPANY

151 Farmington Avenue
Hartford, CT 06156
(203) 273-0123

Aetna Life & Casualty is one of the largest providers of insurance and financial services in the world. With assets of nearly $100 billion, it is also one of the nation's largest corporations.

Despite its size, however, Aetna is one large corporation that truly understands how to keep its employees happy (especially older employees), offering superior benefits, job flexibility and growth opportunities. Openings for job-shares are even posted!

Experience is an EDGE over younger workers!

With the life insurance industry back on the road to financial health job opportunities should continue to grow, particularly in Aetna's HMO segment and within its managed-care health programs.

AMERICAN EXPRESS COMPANY

American Express Tower
World Financial Center
New York, NY 10285
(212) 640-2000

While best known for its Travelers Cheques and American Express Card, American Express has extended its franchise beyond travel and credit cards into insurance, data processing, and publishing. It has long been considered a "blue chip" company with an excellent working environment.

Superior Employee Benefits

American Express pioneered providing employees with such things as family leave programs, elder-care referral, and programs dealing with such topics as wellness.

With nearly 3,000 worldwide locations, American Express continues to provide many full and part-time job opportunities, as well as flexible options such as telecommuting.

Older workers care about the quality of their work!

Jobs will be found not just at corporate headquarters in New York City but at American Express credit card and telemarketing centers throughout the country.

• •

BANKERS TRUST

280 Park Avenue
New York, NY 10017
(212) 250-2500

Bankers Trust represents an ideal corporation for mature workers interested in flexible work schedules and work-at-home opportunities.

A recent **New York Times** article focused on Bankers Trust's personnel policy of recruiting or retraining employees by allowing them greater flex - ibility in their work schedules through "telecommuting." These employees work for a "core" period in the office. The balance of their time is spent at home, connected to their employer via computers, modems, and fax machines.

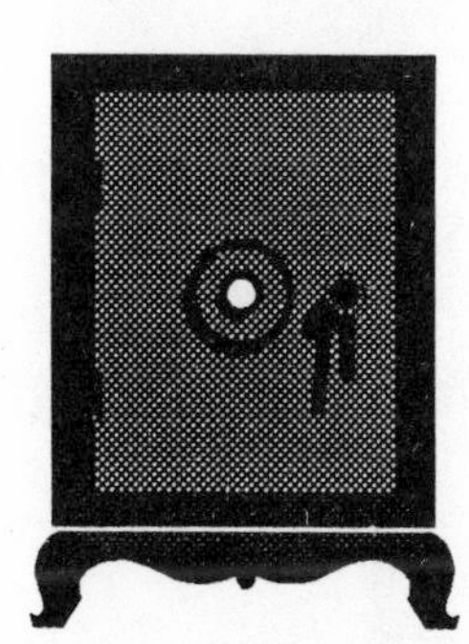

While those with banking experience would be most qualified for positions with Bankers Trust, there are many other good opportunities, within such areas as marketing, accounting, office support positions, and telephone sales.

BARNETT BANKS, INC.

50 North Laura Street
Jacksonville, FL 32202
(904) 791-7720

With 600 offices throughout Florida and Georgia, Barnett Banks is the largest financial institution in Florida, and the ninth largest banking organization in the U.S.

After a recent merger with First Florida Banks and an upturn in the economy, job prospects look especially good at Barnett, particularily for someone considering a second career in the Sunbelt.

Barnett offers many flexible work options, good benefits, and has a strong record in training employees.

• •

CHARLES SCHWAB & COMPANY, INC.

101 Montgomery Street
San Francisco, CA 94104
(415) 627-7000

This highly regarded discount brokerage firm has been growing steadily as individual investors discover the cost advantages of dealing with a top notch discount broker.

Networking helps get jobs!

Superior Customer Service

Charles Schwab's excellent reputation is owing, in large part, to the excellent customer service provided by its employees both through its Tele-Broker service and its retail operation.

The trend toward purchase of common stocks and bonds from finanical service firms such as Charles Schwab, Fidelity Investments, and Quick and Reilly, should mean many more jobs in the future. Most, however, will be part-time or jobs with flexible hours.

• •

CIGNA CORPORATION

One Liberty Place
1650 Market Street
Philadelphia, PA 19103
(215) 761-6087

CIGNA is one of the nation's leading insurance firms. Two of its principal subsidiaries, Connecticut General and Insurance Company of North Amercia, are equally well known.

CIGNA's financial services include a full range of insurance products such as health, life, property and casualty, and disability insurance. With over 150 offices throughout the country it also administers numerous pension and profit sharing programs.

Opportunities For Retired & Partially Retired People

"We provide a full range of flexible work arrangements, including a variety of part-time arrangements which can meet the needs of retired or partially-retired people," says Susan Thomas, Director of CIGNA's Employment Policies and Programs.

"We also offer eldercare services, wellness programs and full medical benefits to regular part-timers who work at least 17 1/2 hours per week."

Age is an asset in the work place!

THE EQUITABLE LIFE ASSURANCE SOCIETY OF THE U.S.

787 Seventh Avenue
New York, NY 10019
(212) 554-1234

The Equitable Life Assurance Society of the U.S. is one of the nation's largest life insurance companies and the main subsidiary of the Equitable Companies, a diversified financial services organization.

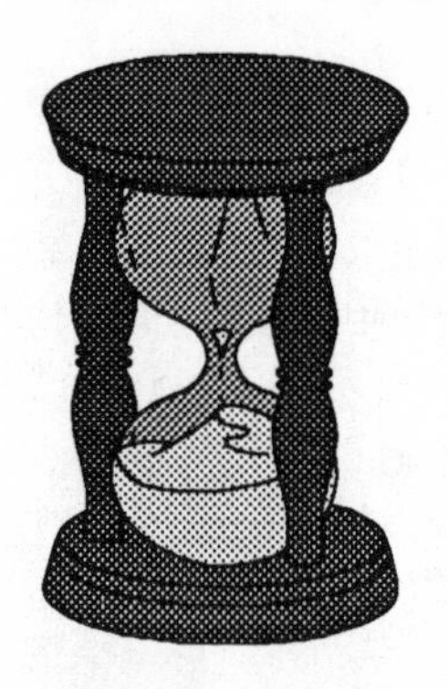

Innovative Hiring Policies

With local offices throughout the country, Equitable is known for its innovative hiring and advancement policies. Equitable has an especially good reputation for hiring and promoting women and minorities.

Equitable hires part-time workers, offers numerous training programs, and is very good about recruiting its own retirees for temporary work and/or special assignments.

STATE FARM MUTUAL AUTOMOBILE INSURANCE COMPANY

One State Farm Plaza
Bloomington, IL 61710
(309) 766-2311

Since 1942, the State Farm Mutual Automobile Insurance Company has been the largest automobile insurance company in the nation. "About one out of every six insured cars on the road is insured with State Farm."

State Farm employs more than 50,000 people who service more than 60 million policies for State Farm customers. It also insures more homes and pleasure boats than any other company, as well as providing property and life insurance through its subsidiaries.

Good Salaries & Benefits

"Starting salaries at State Farm are among the best." Ability, ambition, and performance are key to salary increases and promotions.

State Farm offers on-the-job training, an excellent benefits package, and plenty of promotional opportunities. Their policy is to promote employees from within the organization.

Employment prospects at State Farm are not just limited to the corporate headquarters. State Farm has many regional offices across the U.S.. Current job prospects are strong in areas such as auditing, investments, data processing, and corporate law.

THE TRAVELERS CORPORATION

One Tower Square
Hartford, CT 06183
(203) 277-0111

With offices in all major cities across the U.S., this diversified financial services firm is easily identified by its red umbrella logo.

Travelers is a company that firmly believes in the value of its employees, especially its older workers.

Travelers established an Older Americans Program (Job Bank) more than a decade ago for retirees after finding that many former employees wanted to return to work. They also realized there was a steady need for temporary help, and their former employees fit the bill perfectly!

Travelers offers an excellent benefits package as well as alternative work programs such as job sharing and telecommuting.

• •

WELLS FARGO

420 Montgomery Street
San Francisco, CA 94163
(415) 477-1000

Wells Fargo is a highly regarded California based financial services institution, with over 20,000 employees in more than 500 branch offices throughout the state. It competes with giants such as BankAmerica and Security Pacific.

A very profitable institution, Wells Fargo offers flexible work options, good benefits, elder-care referral services, excellent training and skills upgrading.

Wells Fargo also has a good reputation for hiring and promoting minorities and women.

Health/Pharmaceutical

EMPLOYMENT OUTLOOK

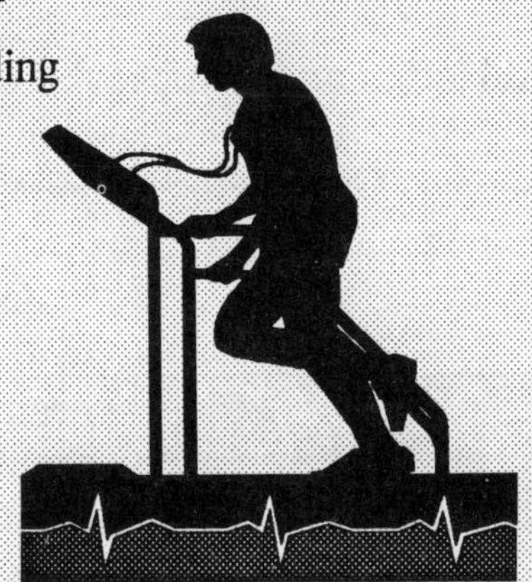

Health-care jobs will continue expanding rapidly as the nation's population gets older and new technologies increase the demand for health services.

Fierce competition, mergers and consolidations, shall continue within the industry as the country awaits a possible complete overhaul of our nation's ailing heath-care system.

Growth areas will be health maintenance organizations, geriatrics, home health care, preventive care, biotechnology.

JOBS IN DEMAND

Biotechnology firms will continue to have job openings for specialized workers. Pharmaceutical corporations and hospitals will hire more part-timers in an effort to adjust their work force to their changing needs.

Best bets: medical technicians, medical assistants, highly trained nurses, pharmaceutical salespeople, management, admnistrative help.

• •

HOFFMANN LA ROCHE, INC.

340 Kingsland Street
Nutley, NJ 07110
(201) 235-5000

Employing close to 20,000 people throughout the United States, this Swiss owned pharmaceutical corporation is best recognized by its famous products such as Librium and Valium. The company is also a majority owner of Genentech, a leading biotechnology firm.

Hoffmann La Roche has an exceptional record for progressive human resources management, including flex-time, job sharing, and child care services.

Part-time Opportunities

At Hoffmann La Roche there is also a corporate tradition of part-time employment among administrative, technical and professional personnel. Overall, the company receives very high marks for "family friendly" policies.

As the American population continues to age, and with a renewed emphasis on health care issues, Hoffmann La Roche should be able to provide ongoing employment opportunities for older workers. Individuals with pharmaceutical sales experience or with backgrounds in chemisty and biotechnology, should receive an especially warm welcome here.

• •

MERCK AND COMPANY, INC.

126 East Lincoln Avenue
Rahway, NJ 07065
(908) 594-4000

Headquartered in Rahway, NJ, Merck is the largest prescription pharmaceutical company in the world. It employs over 30,000 people nationwide and has long been recognized as a company which develops, manufactures, and markets quality health products.

Compensation & Benefits Among Best In Industry

At Merck, there are flexible work policies and substantial rewards for those lucky enough to be hired. Flextime has been in place since the early 1980's, and the pay scale is higher than at most companies in the industry.

Year after year Merck appears on "best company" lists such as FORTUNE's Most Admired Corporations.

To remain ahead of the competition Merck invests nearly $1 billion annually in global research and development. They also have entered into joint ventures with such corporate giants as Du Pont and Johnson & Johnson, thereby increasing employment opportunities in such areas as engineering, computer sciences, sales, and marketing.

● ●

YMCA OF THE USA

101 North Wacker Drive
Chicago, IL 60606
(312) 269-0505

As the nation's largest not-for-profit social service organization with more than 2,000 locations in all 50 states, today's Y offers a wealth of programs and employment opportunities.

"Ys look for people who care about the needs of others," says Karen Blackburn of the Huntington, New York, YMCA. "They want problem solvers, people of compassion."

Flexible Work Options

Ys offer all kinds of career development programs and numerous flexible work options. "They're as diverse as the communities they serve", says Mrs. Blackburn.

HOT GROWTH COMPANIES

EMPLOYMENT OUTLOOK

According to the latest figures from the Bureau of Labor Statistics, by the year 2000, nearly 4 out of 5 jobs will be in industries that provide services.

Business services, particularly personnel supply firms such as Manpower, Olsten, and Kelly, are expected to add the most new jobs as companies face budget cuts and continue hiring temporary workers to handle fluctuating workloads.

Substantial increases in retail employment are also anticipated in restaurants, department stores, and grocery chains. Most government growth will be in state and local government.

JOBS IN DEMAND

While the service sector growth will continue to generate millions of clerical sales and service jobs, it will also create jobs for older professional, technical, and managerial workers, people with previous work experience, training, and educational preparation.

• •

AMERICAN ASSOCIATION OF RETIRED PERSONS

601 E Street, NW
Washington, DC 20049
(202) 434-2277

No organization has done more to dignify the status of older Americans than the AARP. It is also the largest membership organization in the country, carrying out numerous advocacy and educational programs on behalf of senior citizens.

As a source of paid employment, AARP should not be overlooked. While most of the jobs are located in Washinton, DC, AARP has nearly 4000 chapters nationwide and encourages its members to share their knowledge and abilities through AARP's Volunteer Talent Bank. Anyone 50 or over can become an AARP member and the talent bank is an excellent way to network and become more visible in the local community.

Older Workers frequently under value themselves!

AARP publishes what may be the largest circulated periodicals in America: **Modern Maturity** and **AARP Bulletin**. They also administer a number of programs in conjunction with leading American corporations. For example, AARP's travel club partner is American Express. Bank One runs the AARP VISA card program and the Hartford Insurance Company is the business partner for auto and homeowners' insurance programs.

Questions regarding employment with AARP should be addressed to AARP's Washington headquarters.

THE ARA GROUP, INC.

1101 Market Street
Philadelphia, PA 19107
(215) 238-3000

Headquartered in Philadelphia, ARA is one of the largest food service companies in the U.S. Each day they provide food and leisure services to more than 12 million people, businesses, schools, hospitals, convention centers, and governments.

Other ARA divisions provide such diverse services as health and family care services, magazine and book distribution, uniform rental, and janitorial services. ARA's 140,000 employees work in more than 700 different job classifications, from gourmet cooks to childhood development specialists and truck drivers!

ARA continues to expand, offering many different job opportunities, advancement, training, and flexibility.

• •

BEN & JERRY'S HOMEMADE, INC.

Post Office Box 240
Waterbury, VT 05676
(802) 244-6957

Ben & Jerry's is known nationwide for its rich high quality ice cream The entire corporation was founded on values that combine old fashioned entrepreneurism and high-minded social values.

This is a company that commits 7.5% of its pre-tax profits to charity, and channels money toward preservation of the Amazon Rain Forest through sales of its "Rainforest Crunch" ice cream.

Work Here Is Fun

Progressive employment practices characterizes Ben & Jerry's. Work here is fun, benefits are good, and the needs of its diverse group of employees are always of major importance.

Look for job opportunities and flexible work options at any of its increasing franchise operations, or at the company's headquarters in Vermont.

As a result of its ability to develop and market successful new flavors, Ben & Jerry's is about to pass leader Haagen-Dazs in market share!

BLOCKBUSTER ENTERTAINMENT

One Blockbuster Plaza
Fort Lauderdale, FL 33301
(305) 832-3000

"Grandaddy of video rental chains"

With more than 3,000 domestic outlets, Blockbuster is the largest video chain retailer in the U.S!

Blockbuster is working to become a global brand name in entertainment. It entered the music industry by recently acquiring the Sound Warehouse and Music Plus chains, and is seriously looking to develop a chain of very large music retail stores in the U.S., Europe, and Australia with the British company, Virgin.

Blockbuster also wants to become a major player in the distribution and production of filmed entertainment, which will open up many jobs in areas such as sales, promotion, and service.

• •

R.R. DONNELLEY & SONS COMPANY

2223 Martin Luther King Drive
Chicago, IL 60616
(312) 326-8000

R.R. Donnelley is the world's largest printer, specializing in books, catalogues, computer documentation, directories, and financial documentation. Founded in 1864, Donnelley employs over 31,000 people and offers full in-house services, from creative to presort mailing. Annual sales are over $3 billion and they operate manufacturing, sales, and operations facilities worldwide.

Donnelley wants workers who can respond to the needs of its customers! The company has an excellent comprehensive benefits package, and offers all kinds of flexible work options in such areas as engineering, computer systems, marketing, manufacturing, and sales.

H.B. FULLER COMPANY

2400 Energy Park Drive
St. Paul, MN 55108
(612) 645-3401

H.B. Fuller is NOT like other chemical companies. This specialty chemicals manufacturer is dedicated to its employees and to protecting the environment. The company promises all employees that if their job becomes obsolete, Fuller will retrain them in a new technology.

Fuller also boasts one of the best records in the chemical industry. It has established an environmental, health, and safety policy to which all plants and labs must adhere.

Fuller encourages people to become involved in community activities at its 34 plant locations. Employees are paid to take up to 12 hours off each quarter to work in a community organization or project.

Fuller still gives employees the day off on their birthday and there are generous rewards for veteran employees.

• •

THE HOME DEPOT, INC.

2727 Paces Ferry Road
Atlanta, GA 30339
(404) 433-8211

USA's Largest Home-improvement Retailer

Founded in 1978, this Atlanta based home improvement chain has "revolutionized" the home do-it-yourself industy.

With over 225 stores that are 2 to 3 times the size of the average home center store, Home Depot offers huge inventories and low prices. It is no wonder they are No. 1 in the $100 billion home improvement industry, and growing bigger and bigger each year!

While Many Are Floundering, Home Depot Is Thriving

Home Depot has become an excellent source of full and part-time jobs, especially for customer service oriented individuals. Unlike other retailers, Home Depot has actually been thriving during the recent recession, adding more stores and employees as more and more people seek to save money by doing their own home improvements.

Emphasize what skills and experiences you have!

Home Depot's goal is to have at least 500 stores by 1996. Their next big growth areas: Washington, D.C. and the Midwest.

KELLY SERVICES, INC.

999 West Big Beaver
Troy, MI 48084
(313) 362-4444

Offices In All Major U.S. Cities

Kelly Services is a nationwide temporary employment agency which provides temporary office, marketing, light industrial, and home service care to a diversified group of customers through local offices in every major city in the U.S.

Each year Kelly hires over 500,000 employees for customers involved in industry, government, commerce, and professional offices (e.g. accountants, attorneys, and physicians.)

More Executives Serve As Temporary Employees

In the late 1980's Kelly instituted a program specifically aimed at recruiting older workers, finding that they were especially ideal for part-time opportunities and short-term assignments. Today, more and more companies are hiring temporary employees to handle fluctuating workloads.

Older workers must keep their skills up to date!

"We provide substitute workers for anyone who isn't there!" said one Kelly officer.

• •

KINKO'S COPY CENTERS

P.O. Box 8000
Ventura, CA 93002
(805) 652-4000

Jobs Available!

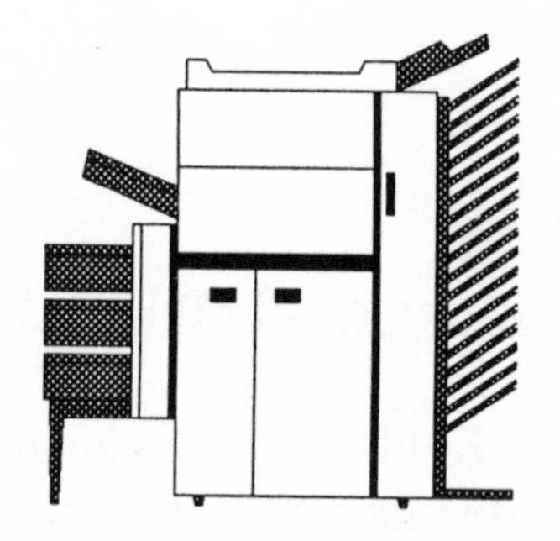

Mature workers in search of part-time, flexible work schedules, take note: there are close to 1,000 Kinko's Copy Centers throughout the U.S., providing employment for many thousands of full and part-time customer service representatives.

Kinko's was originally established to service the copying needs of students. The first stores were located on, or near California campuses. Kinko's differentiates itself by the levels of copy services it provides. Most are open 24 hours a day!

In addition to plain, white paper copying, Kinko's handles binding, passport photos, mounting, fax services, blueprints and desktop publishing. They can even create resume packages, including laser typesetting and envelopes.

Kinko's is especially interested in hiring Store Managers and Assistant Managers. They want people with previous supervisory experience, those who understand customer service, candidates who enjoy working with other people.

MANPOWER, INC.

5301 North Ironwood Road
Milwaukee, WI 53217
(414) 961-1000

Many Temporary Jobs!

With offices in virtually every major city in the world, Manpower is the largest nongovernmental temporary employment services organization in the world.

Working on a temporary basis can be an excellent way to get an "overview" of the many different types of job opportunities that are available within a particular geographical area. For the mature worker, Manpower is a very good place to find a flexible or part-time position.

Temporary workers are becoming more and more important in our work force. Each year Manpower assigns nearly 2 million workers to jobs in corporations of all kinds, large and small.

McDONALD'S CORPORATION

McDonald's Plaza
Oak Brook, IL 60521
(708) 575-3000

LUNCHTIME

With nearly 15,000 restaurants worldwide, McDonald's is, indeed, the world's largest food service organization.

McMasters Program

McDonald's is especially keen on hiring older workers. Not long ago they began a program called "McMasters," whereby they provide special classroom training, supervised work experience, and job placement for older employees. They'll even let retirees define their own work hours!

With plans to build 400 to 500 new restaurants each year (especially in non-traditional markets such as hospitals, airports, and shopping malls) McDonald's continues to be an excellent source for full-time, part-time, and flex-time job opportunities.

• •

OLSTEN CORPORATION

One Merrick Avenue
Westbury, NY 11590
(516) 832-8200

Founded in 1950, Olsten is a nationwide temporary employment agency with offices in major cities throughout the U.S.

Like other temporary employment agencies, Olsten provides part-time work for specific periods of time to a wide variety of large and small corporations.

Need For Professional Temps!

While temporary help agencies used to be restricted to clerical and secretarial needs, there is now a need for professional level temporary help, especially in such areas as accounting and marketing. Olsten currently has expanded into health care services, recognizing the tremendous growth taking place in this industry and the need for supplemental hospital and nursing home staffing.

> **Jobs go to those who sell themselves best!**

As American corporations continue to "downsize" and the need for a flexible workforce continues to increase, agencies such as Olsten will continue to provide a great deal of flexible work opportunities.

• •

ROBERT HALF INTERNATIONAL, INC.

2884 Sand Hill Road
Menlo Park, CA 94025
(415) 854-9700

World's Largest Financial Personnel Services Firm

Robert Half is the world's largest financial personnel services firm. It operates nearly 200 offices under its Robert Half and Accountemps trade names and specializes in the permanent and temporary placement of accounting, financial, and data processing, and banking professionals.

Robert Half services many different types of large and small corporations and for mature workers continues to be an excellent source of flexible, part-time, job opportunities. Check the yellow pages for the local branch office nearest you.

STAPLES, INC.

100 Pennsylvania Avenue
Framingham, MA 01701
(508) 370-8500

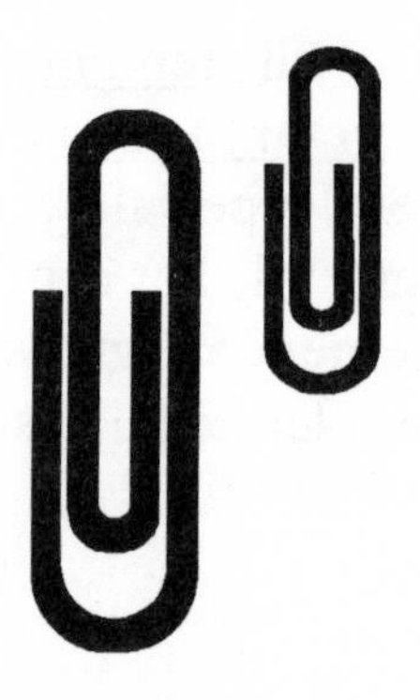

Staples pioneered the concept of "The Office Superstore," when it opened its first store in 1986. It currently operates nearly 200 high-volume office superstores in more than 15 states, selling everything from "paper clips to computers".

Each Staples store stocks some 5,000 items but customers may special order approximately 20,000 other items. Discounts range from 30% to 70% off catalog list price.

Staples offers job opportunities in its corporate office, distribution centers, and in all of its store locations. Staples continues to expand aggressively, creating opportunities for project managers, store managers, and assistant managers.

• •

TCBY ENTERPRISES

425 West Capitol Avenue
Little Rock, AR 72201
(501) 688-8229

TCBY (The Country's Best Yogurt) is the largest franchiser of soft serve frozen yogurt in the U.S. Its nearly 1,700 stores are located in free standing locations, shopping centers and in shopping malls.

Age proof your resume

With plans to expand into locations such as airports, theme parks, and sports stadiums, TCBY continues to look for managers, marketers, and sales people, offering very good benefits and flexible work options.

TOYS 'R' US

461 From Road
Paramus, NJ 07652
(201) 262-7800

Nation's Largest Toy Retailer

With nearly 25% of the U.S. toy market, Toys 'R' Us is the nation's largest toy retailer. The company currently operates over 500 Toys 'R' Us toy stores in 44 states and 200 Kids 'R' Us retail clothing stores.

Toys 'R' Us is known for its computer inventory system which allows employees to meticulously monitor inventory amounts and needs at each store.

Job Openings!

"Agressive expansion" of both domestic and international toy operations and the clothing division, as well as new instore Children's Book Shops, means Toys 'R' Us will continue to gain market share and be a good employment source for the future.

• •

U.S. GOVERNMENT

Despite all of the talk about shrinking the size of government and reducing the federal deficit, Uncle Sam is, and probably always will be, one of this country's biggest employers.

Federal employees have opportunities, benefits, and challenges few private industry employers can provide or match! There are nearly 150 departments and independent agencies to choose from, national issues to deal with, and all sorts of training programs, seminars, and opportunities available. No one is limited to one specific organization, occupation, or geographical area either.

No Age discrimination!

Best of all, hiring and promotion are based strictly on qualifications and effective performance. The federal government really does bend over backwards not to discriminate on the basis of age.

The best way to start your federal job hunt is to look through the "Blue Pages" of your local telephone directory. Most large cities have an Office of Personnel Management Service Center, and the telephone number and address will be listed there.

Commercial publications such as **Federal Jobs Digest** and **Federal Career Opportunities** are available in most libraries or at newsstands. Another very helpful book is **Government Job Finder** by Daniel Lauber.

• •

WAL-MART STORES

702 Southwest Eighth Street
Bentonville, AR 72716
(501) 273-4000

One Of Largest Employers In The U.S.

The late Sam Walton was one of the great geniuses of modern American Capitalism. The Wal-Mart chain is fast approaching 2,000 stores, and there is no end in sight to the level of expansion.

Wal-Mart employs close to 400,000 people. The sheer magnitude of the Wal-Mart operation makes it one of the nation's major employers.

Wal-Mart has been successful because it treats its employees extremely well, and also because it is very very attentive to customer service.

Most jobs are on the selling floor for sales representatives or cashiers. Other employment can be found in Wal-Mart's distribution and warehousing operations.

Companies always want competent professionals

Wal-Mart's New Supercenters

Wal-Mart may soon be one of the largest grocers in the nation! The company has opened a number of Supercenters: a typical Wal-Mart merchandise store and a full-size grocery store combined.

WENDY'S INTERNATIONAL, INC.

4288 West Dublin-Granville Road
Dublin, OH 43017
(614) 764-3100

With over 4,000 restaurant operations in 49 states and in 23 foreign countries, Wendy's is the third largest restaurant chain in the world.

Special Training For Older Workers

Like industry leader McDonalds, Wendy's is especially open to hiring older workers. Wendy's provides special training, supervised work experiences, and job placement. Wendy's even allows retirees to define their own work hours.

With plans to have open over 5,000 outlets by the year 1995, Wendy's offers good employment prospects, good salaries and benefits, and plenty of flexible work options.

Media and Entertainment

EMPLOYMENT OUTLOOK

The media/entertainment industry is changing rapidly, creating all sorts of new possibilities and exciting new job opportunities.

Huge entertainment, communications, and information companies are merging (or else looking for alliances) as the development of new media and communications technology forms what has been called "**the information highway.**"

Employment opportunities within the publishing/newspaper industry will depend largely upon the particular company. Continuing consolidation and competition will mean most new jobs will come from attrition.

JOBS IN DEMAND

As the American population gets older it will have more money to spend on leisure time activities.. Look for entertainment giants such as Walt Disney to continue expanding, offering many good job opportunti

GANNETT COMPANY, INC.

1100 Wilson Boulevard
Arlington, VA 22234
(703) 284-6000

Gannett is the largest U.S. newspaper company, with 81 daily newspapers, including **USA Today**, and more than 50 non-daily publications.

Known for its diverse workforce, Gannett is involved in research, marketing, commercial printing, data services, and news programming.

Older workers mean lower turnover!

Women And Minorities

Long considered an industry leader in hiring and promoting women and minorities (Black Enterprise magazine named Gannett one of the best places for blacks to work), Gannett's training programs and benefits are excellent.

• •

KNIGHT-RIDDER, INC.

One Herald Plaza
Miami, FL 33132
(305) 376-3800

Knight-Ridder (formerly Knight-Ridder Newspapers, Inc.) is a newspaper publishing and information services company.

Knight-Ridder publishes nearly 30 daily newspapers, including the **Miami Herald, Philadephia Inquirer**, and **Detroit Free Press**, making it one of the largest newspaper chains in the U.S.

While Knight-Ridder employs over 20,000 people, it has long had a reputation for being committed to equal opportunity for its employees, pushing for the advancement of women and minorities.

Training and individual growth are extremely important here. Knight-Ridder's newspaper training school offers a wide variety of training seminars.

While Knight-Ridder's newpaper business continues to grow at a moderate rate, it is the systems and cable operations that are currently expanding rapidly and offering excellent opportunities for many different jobs.

• •

PUBLISHERS CLEARING HOUSE

382 Channel Drive
Port Washington, NY 11050
(516) 883-5432

Located in Port Washington, New York, Publishers Clearing House is a direct marketing company known by tens of millions of people who respond regularly each year to its famous sweepstakes.

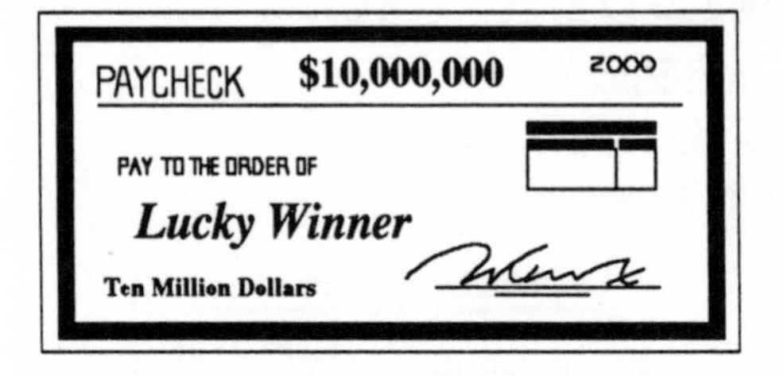

The familiar manila envelope offers discounted magazine subscriptions, and a chance to win big bucks and make a dream come true.

Besides magazines, Publishers Clearing House promotes many other products and services, such as books, tapes, music, and useful household items. The Power Line, their telemarketing operation, also specializes in business to business and business to consumer campaigns.

Publishers Clearing House offers excellent salaries, benefits, and opportunities for promotion. It hires many temporary part-time employees, especially during peak sweepstakes mailing periods (2-4 times each year). Plus, its telemarketing division is always looking to hire good telemarketing sales reps.

TIME WARNER, INC.

75 Rockefeller Plaza
New York, NY 10019
(212) 484-8000

Largest Media And Entertainment Company

The merger of Time, Inc. and Warner Communications, Inc. in 1989 produced the largest media and entertainment company in the world. Magazines such as Time, People, Fortune, Money, and Sports Illustrated are all part of the Time Warner empire.

Time Warner also owns Book of the Month Club, Little Brown & Co., and DC Comics, Inc. It is also the leading music company in the world. Home Box Office is probably the best known of its broadcasting properties. Its Six Flags amusement parks offer excellent seasonal employment opportunities.

Good Work Environment

Part-time work, job-sharing, and work-at-home are becoming traditional at this communications giant. The work environment is excellent and, because of its size, opportunities almost limitless.

New Opportunities

Time Warner's recent partnership with US West should mean all sorts of new markets and even more job opportunities are about to unfold! Customers could, in the very near future, get local cable and telephone service from the same source, sort of like "One Stop Shopping" for subscribers.

WALT DISNEY COMPANY

500 South Buena Vista Street
Burbank, CA 91521
(818) 560-1000

The success of Disney is one of the great legends of American business. The current generation of executive leadership has ambitious growth plans, and this should translate into all sorts of wonderful opportunities throughout the vast entertainment corporation.

Continued Expansion

Disney continues to expand its amusement parks, hotels, film, television, books and magazine publishing, and its extremely popular Disney retail store outlets.

There are always opportunities for qualified part-time workers. Recent newspaper ads have appeared looking to fill jobs as varied as accountants, data analysts, and operations schedulers.

New Resorts, New Jobs!

Most jobs will continue to be located at Disney's theme parks in Florida and in southern California. (Just recently Disney announced plans to build three new resorts in Walt Disney World in Florida, as well as a third water theme park.) The company is enormous, however, and there are many other job opportunites in places such as Kansas and New Jersey.

Retail/Mail-Order

EMPLOYMENT OUTLOOK

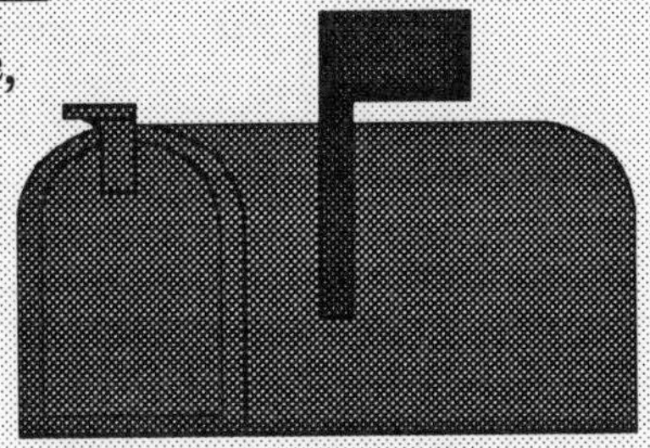

As the economy continues to improve, competition within the retail/mail-order industries will remain high. Good management will be crucial! Only the strongest and most innovative companies will survive as department stores, specialty and discount stores, and mail-order companies fight to attract customers.

Super discount stores are becoming a major source of new employment, offering hourly pay and very good benefits. New technology is changing the way many companies do business. Some retailers, such as Nordstrom, see the future in interactive television.

Mail-order companies will continue to seek ways to target their customer and gain market share.

JOBS IN DEMAND

Best bets: sales people, buyers, merchandisers, telemarketers, customer service people.

• •

CURRENT, INC.

P.O. Box 2559
Colorado Springs, CO 80901
(719) 594-4100

Acquired in 1987 by Deluxe Corporation, Current is the largest direct mail marketer of consumer specialty products in the U.S. It distributes greeting cards, calendars, gift wrap, small gifts, and related accessories.

Current also is a "major specialty printer", producing in-house two-thirds of its more than 2,000 products! Its low cost printing and distribution systems helps give Current an important price advantage over its retail competitors.

Companies want people who can wear more than one hat!

As market conditions improve, Current continues to develop and test new products, institute special sales promotions, and expand its market share.

Best bets for future jobs: sales, marketing, customer service, administrative services.

● ●

DAYTON HUDSON CORPORATION

777 Nicollet Mall
Minneapolis, MN 55402
(612) 370-6948

Dayton Hudson is one of the great retailing giants with over 800 stores nationwide. They range from discount stores such as Target and Mervyn's, to more elegant department stores

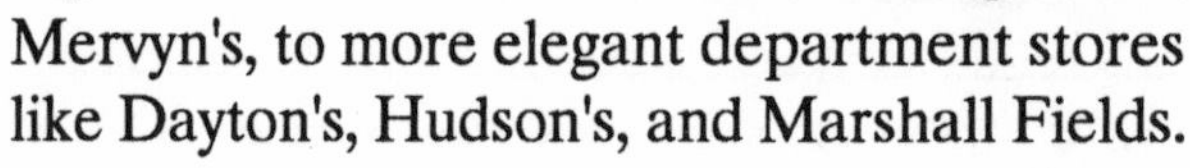

like Dayton's, Hudson's, and Marshall Fields.

Lots of Opportunities!

Dayton Hudson offers a full range of opportunities, both part-time and full-time. There is also plenty of opportunity for individual growth. Benefits are "family friendly".

With future plans calling for many more store openings (particularly the highly successful Target super store format), Dayton Hudson will continue to be filling positions within nearly all divisions.

• •

EDDIE BAUER

15010 NE 36th Street
Redmond, WA 98052
(206) 882-6100

Long known for its high quality, rugged outdoor wear, Eddie Bauer continues to enjoy the prosperity and growth that has characterized the direct marketing industry.

Unlike L.L. Bean, Eddie Bauer has diversified into retail sales. Its stores are found in upscale shopping areas in nearly every major city in America, offering good full and part-time sales positions.

Opportunites in telemarketing and warehouse distribution will also continue at the Eddie Bauer Seattle headquarters.

• •

HONEY BAKED HAM COMPANY, INC.

635 Kingsbridge Road
Carrollton, GA 30117
(404) 836-5900

A family owned and operated business, Honey Baked Ham Company has been around ever since Harry J. Hoenselaar opened his first store in 1957 and introduced his infamous "spiral sliced HoneyBaked Ham".

With a strong dedication to quality and customer satisfaction, the company has continued to grow and prosper. Today, there are now over 200 Honey Baked stores in 35 states. Customers may also call a toll-free number and Honey Baked will ship one of many ready-to-serve items anywhere in the U.S!

"Service jobs are everywhere!"

With the company continuing to open new stores, look for job opportunities and flexible work options at any of its locations. Best job bets: management, sales, customer service.

J.C. PENNEY COMPANY, INC.

14841 North Dallas Parkway
Dallas, TX 75240
(214) 591-1000

J.C. Penney, like Kmart and Sears, is one of America's retailing giants. It too is a fertile source of professional and part-time jobs.

J.C. Penney has over 200,000 employees and more than 2,500 department stores throughout the country. A large number of employees work as "seasonal sales associates", or on a part-time basis.

In addition to its retail operation, J.C. Penney has a large catalog and telemarketing division. (With 16 telemarketing centers nationwide, this is the fastest growing area of the catalog division).

J.C. Penney also operates an insurance company and owns several hundred drug stores, all of which are hiring full and part-time people.

• •

THE KROGER COMPANY

1014 Vine Street
Cincinnati, OH 45202
(513) 762-4000

Cincinnati-based Kroger is the nation's largest grocery chain. Known for its generous incentive bonus plan, it continues to be a good source of jobs, operating 1,300 supermarkets in 24 states and 1,000 convenience stores in 16 states. Several well-known Kroger operated convenience stores include: Thom Thumb, Kwik Shop, and Turkey Hill Minit Markets.

In order to increase market share, Kroger intends to develop new store locations, as well as emphasize the over 4,000 private label products it manufactures at its own 37 processing plants.

• •

LANDS' END, INC.

Lands' End Lane
Dodgeville, WI 53595
(608) 935-9341

Lands' End started 30 years ago as a Chicago based supplier of sailing equipment. Today, Lands' End is one of the most prestigious mail order firms in the nation, rivaling L.L. Bean in its level of sales and the quality of its customer service. The company is frequently mentioned on lists of America's best corporations. A great reminder of this nation's entrepreneurial spirit, Lands' End went public in 1986.

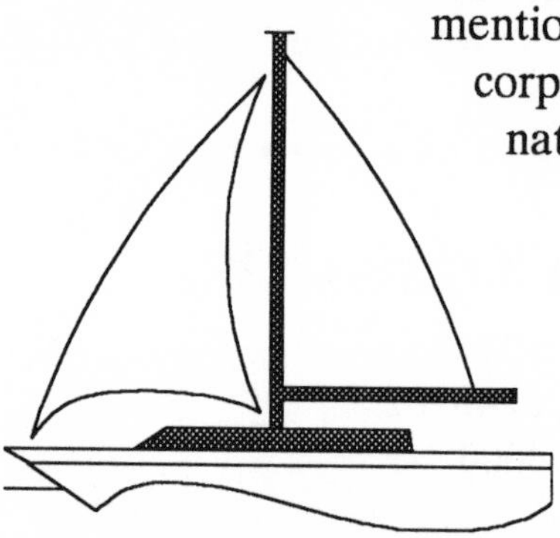

Since the trend toward mail order buying shows no sign of letting up, the job outlook at Lands' End remains bright.

Good full and part-time jobs are available at Lands' End's Dodgeville headquarters, and at its outlet stores (located in the Midwest).

• •

THE LIMITED, INC.

Two Limited Parkway
Columbus, OH 43216
(614) 479-7000

With over 4,000 stores nationwide, The Limited is one of the country's largest companies specializing in women's apparel. This highly successful retail chain includes such well-known stores as Victoria's Secret (intimate apparel), Lane Bryant (fashions for the larger-sized woman), Limited Stores (medium priced fashion apparel).

The Limited manufactures most of its goods, operates a bank that issues its own credit cards, and runs several catalog operations (Brylane Catalog and Victoria's Secret).

Acquisitions And Opportunities

As The Limited continues to grow bigger through acquisitions, such as Abercrombie & Fitch, and the economy grows stronger, full and part-time job opportunities shall continue to be in good supply at this ambitious, exciting, company. Recent company needs include: Art Director, Production Specialist, and Freelance Graphic designers.

L.L. BEAN, INC.

Casco Street
Freeport, ME 04033
(207) 865-4761

During its long history, L.L. Bean has earned a reputation as one of the most highly regarded firms in the $200 billion mail-order industry.

Employees take great pride in working for this privately owned New England-based retail and catalog merchandiser of outdoor sporting equipment and apparel. Virtually all 4,000 employees work at the company headquarters in Freeport, Maine. Pay and benefits are good, and annual turnover is very low.

As the growth of the mail-order industry continues, the best bets for jobs will be in these areas: catalog development, customer service, and warehousing. L.L. Bean hires many part-timers during the busy holiday season. Recently L.L. Bean has advertised for experienced professionals such as data analysts and senior business analysts.

• •

MELVILLE CORPORATION

One Theall Road
Rye, NY 10580
(914) 925-4000

With nearly 9,000 stores in all 50 states, Melville Corporation is one of the largest and most diverse specialty retailers in the country.

A highly regarded company, Melville's product lines include apparel, footwear, health and beauty supplies, toys, and household furnishings. Its stores include such well-known chains as CVS, Thom McAn, Marshalls, Kay-Bee, Chess King, and Meldisco.

Despite a soft economy, Melville has continued to grow (primarily through acquisitons), adding a wide variety of full and part-time sales positions. Management has also been very adept at starting new chains that seem to offer national sales potential.

Don't be afraid to take risks!

Stores and support facilities are being continually updated in order to better meet the needs of its customers, as well as to stay ahead of the competition.

NORDSTROM, INC.

1501 Fifth Avenue
Seattle, WA 98101
(206) 628-2111

Customers

Nordstrom is a Seattle headquartered department store chain which caters to upscale customers and has a reputation for providing superior levels of customer service. It is famous for sending personal thank you notes to its customers. At Nordstom, it seems, "the customer really is always right".

Catering To Upscale Customers

With over 30,000 employees, Nordstrom operates 70 stores in nine states, offering elegant clothing, shoes, and accessories. It also has 16 clearance stores.

Most Nordstrom employees work as if they owned the store! Nearly all sales representatives work on a commission basis, and the company helps instill loyalty by promoting only from within.

Nordstrom continues to renovate stores and is working hard to develop a catalog operation. It is also planning to be a major player in "interactive television".

SAFEWAY, INC.

Fourth and Jackson Streets
Oakland, CA 94660
(415) 891-3000

Large supermarket chains like Safeway can frequently solve the part-time employment needs of the older worker.

Safeway is one of the world's largest food retailers and currently operates over 1,100 stores in the U.S. and Canada.

The company is currently in the midst of a five year $3.2 billion capital spending program, and continues to build and remodel stores for future growth.

SEARS, ROEBUCK & COMPANY

Sears Tower
Chicago, IL 60684
(312) 875-2500

Despite recent restructuring Sears continues to be a good source of part-time and seasonal jobs for seniors. The giant retailer discontinued its 97 year old unprofitable catalog operation, restructured its financial services unit, and overhauled its merchandise division. Sears has gone back to what it knows best: retailing and its customers!

Sears' repositioning seems to be working. Earnings are up and customers are back. Even the stock market has given it the thumbs up!

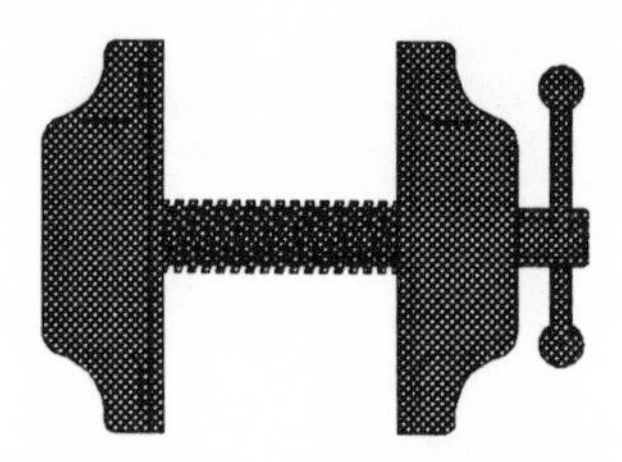

Sears is spending $4 billion to increase the amount of store space dedicated to clothing, accessories, and makeup. It is de-emphasizing hard goods (hardware and appliances). Women with families are now the main target customers of a more "focused" Sears.

WALGREEN COMPANY

200 Wilmot Road
Deerfield, IL 60015
(708) 940-2500

Growth and opportunity will continue for Walgreen, the largest drugstore chain in the U.S., as the nation's population grows older and the demand for prescription drugs increases.

Change tactics if you're not getting results!

Nearly 10% Of The Nation's Prescriptions

Walgreen currently operates some 2,000 stores in 30 states, serving 2 million customers every day. With health-care reform expected to increase sales of prescription drugs, Walgreen plans to open approximately 200 new stores each year.

WINN-DIXIE STORES, INC.

5050 Edgewood Court
Jacksonville, FL 32205
(904) 783-5000

Winn-Dixie is the largest food retailer in the Sunbelt with 1,200 stores in 13 Southeastern states. The company also operates a network of 16 distribution centers, 27 processing and manufacturing plants, and a fleet of delivery trucks, all of which translates into numerous full and part-time job opportunities.

This Jacksonville, Florida-based chain continues to make improvements. Recently it launched an "everyday low-price campaign", computerized its trucking fleet, and opened high profit specialty departments.

With plans to open 50-100 new stores in the next few years and to remodel or enlarge many others, Winn-Dixie is positioned for steady earnings growth and should remain an excellent source of new jobs.

Transportation and Hospitality

EMPLOYMENT OUTLOOK

Employment within the transportation industry is expected to rise slightly. Freight Forwarding, the fastest growing division, should continue to see the most job growth.

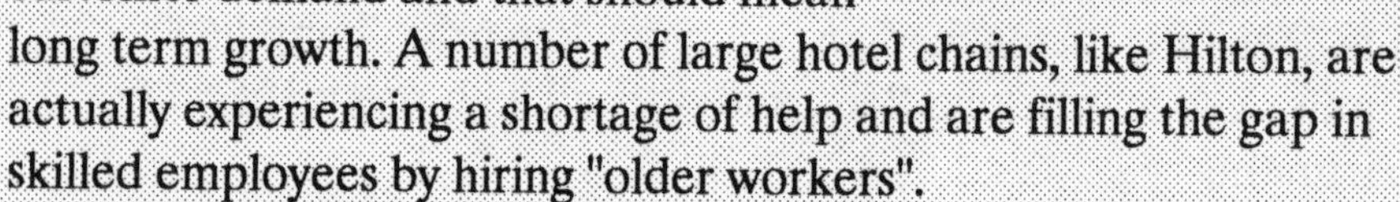

The hospitality and travel industry is beginning to experience greater customer demand and that should mean long term growth. A number of large hotel chains, like Hilton, are actually experiencing a shortage of help and are filling the gap in skilled employees by hiring "older workers".

As the population continues to get older, look for more corporations such as Marriott to become involved in services aimed at the elderly.

JOBS IN DEMAND

Best bets: management, customer service, food service, marketing, elder care.

• •

AIRBORNE FREIGHT CORPORATION

3101 Western Avenue
Seattle, WA 98111
(206) 285-4600

Airborne is an air express carrier that delivers small packages, documents, and heavy freight throughout the U.S. and to over 200 other countries worldwide. It is one of the nation's fastest growing employers.

Known for a wide variety of automated programs and services, Airborne "...has one of the lowest costs per shipment of any carrier in the industry." Employee productivity is one of the primary reasons.

Airborne continues to use aggressive marketing, a low cost structure, and a highly trained sales force to get more business and increase market share. "Our goal is not to force customers into our mode of operation; but instead, to adapt our systems to those of our customers." Airborne is a well-known source of part-time jobs.

• •

AMR CORPORATION

P.O. Box 619616
Dallas-Fort Worth Airport
Fort Worth, TX 75261
(817) 963-1234

American Airlines, the largest subsidiary of Fort Worth based AMR Corporation, is one company that doesn't care how old you are, only that you can do the job.

Always expect success!

"We have a recruitment drive aimed specifically at hiring mature candidates", boasts Kim Williams, Product Manager. "Because of the diversity of our passengers, for example, we've hired hundreds of 40+ flight attendants."

Even better job opportunities can be found at four of AMR's non-airline divisions:

o **Sabre Travel Information Network**-the world's largest privately owned reservation and travel data processing system.

- **AMR Services**-provides ground handling and ground transportation for other airlines.
- **AMR Information Services**-provides information management services to other airlines and data processing for the travel industry.
- **American Airlines Decision Technologies**-develops software packages and computer systems.

"The pay and benefits are excellent within the AMR organization,", says Ms. Williams, "plus, there are lots of opportunities for flextime".

AVIS, INC.

900 Old Country Road
Garden City, NY 11530
(516) 222-3000

Avis is a leader in the car rental services field and one of the largest employee-owned companies in the U.S.

In 1987, Avis employees established an ESOP (employee stock ownership plan) and bought the company for $1.75 billion. As a result, every Avis employee receives a certain number of shares of stock based on the company's profits.

Owning the company provides employees with job security. The pay, benefits, and opportunities are all very good. Promotion usually comes from within and there are numerous job opportunities, including hourly positions such as rental sales agents and shuttle bus drivers.

With over 5,000 locations (25% of which are in airports) Avis is poised to overtake industry leader Hertz Corporation.

CARLSON COMPANIES, INC.

Carlson Parkway
P.O. Box 59159
Minneapolis, MN 55459
(612) 540-5452

Minneapolis based Carlson Companies, Inc. is the parent of a diversified, world wide group of business enterprises operating primarily in the area of hospitality and travel. The company is probably best known for its Radisson Hotels International, Colony Hotels & Resorts, and Country Lodging Inns. The Carlson Hospitality Group also operates the popular Country Kitchen and T.G. I. Friday's restaurant chains. The Carlson Marketing Group is one of the largest marketing firms in the world, with offices in most major American cities.

The firm now employs more than 100,000 people and should continue to add jobs throughout the rest of the decade and beyond. New Radisson Hotels open regularly and the company just recently launched its own cruise ship, the Radisson Diamond.

• •

CARNIVAL CRUISE LINES, INC.

Carnival Place
3655 NW 87th Avenue
Miami, FL 33178
(305) 599-2600

The general increase in leisure time as well as the "graying" of America has benefited the travel industry tremendously. Carnival Cruise Lines is now the largest cruise operator in the country. It employs close to 20,000 people, and the long term outlook is for more growth.

The key to Carnival's success has been its diversification into different market segments throughout the travel industry. Customer service positions are critical in this type of business, as are marketing jobs. Employee opportunities continue to expand at its Miami headquarters, as well as aboard the various ships in Carnival's fleet.

DAYS INN

339 Jefferson Road
Parsippany, NJ 07054
(201) 428-9700

Days Inn, one of the largest hotel chains in America, was recently the subject of a case study on the advantages of hiring workers over 55. The study was part of a project completed by the Commonwealth Fund of New York as part of its Americans Over 55 at Work Program.

In 1986, Days Inn started to actively recruit and hire older workers for its computerized reservations center in Atlanta. The company quickly learned that older workers helped reduce turnover dramatically.

Days Inn also found that mature workers were better sales people. Absenteeism plummeted and, because older workers were on the job longer, recruitment and training costs also fell off sharply.

The hospitality and travel industry, despite short term recessionary trends, has a healthy long term growth outlook. Days Inn, as well as other hotels and motels throughout the country should continue to be good sources of employment for older workers. Customer service positions, such as those in reservations centers, should be particularly good areas for those seeking employment.

• •

FEDERAL EXPRESS CORPORATION

2005 Corporate Avenue
Memphis, TN 38132
(901) 369-3600

Headquartered in Memphis, Federal Express is the largest private overnight delivery service in the U.S., delivering nearly 1.5 million packages daily. In 1989 it acquired Flying Tigers to become the largest all-cargo airline.

Federal Express is an "employee-oriented company". It is one place that truly puts people ahead of profit. Promotion is from within and there is an extensive in-house training program.

Federal Express has long been known for its flextime policy and Guaranteed Fair Treatment, and no-layoff policy.

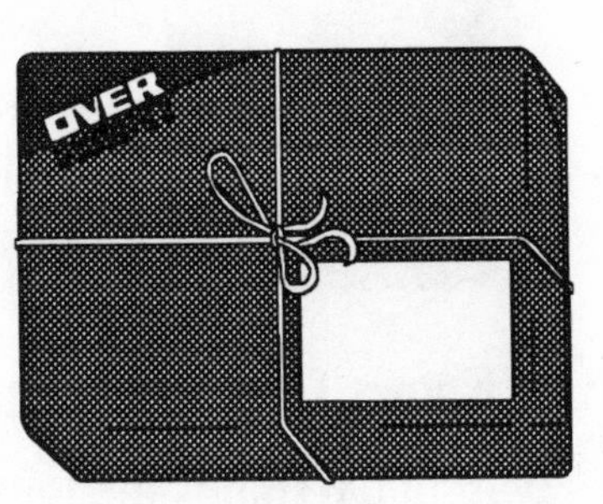

Pay, benefits, and opportunites are all very good at Federal Express. Plus, the company hires many part-timers.

• •

HILTON HOTELS CORPORATION

9336 Civic Center Drive
Beverly Hills, CA 90209
(310) 278-4321

With over 100,000 rooms in over 200 U.S. cities, Hilton is one of America's biggest hotel operators.

But Hilton is no longer just a hotel company! A large portion of its operating income now comes from its five hotel-casinos in Nevada, and it is planning to expand its gaming business. Under consideration are riverboat casinos in such states as Missouri and Louisiana.

Shortage Of Workers

Like many other hotels in the industry, Hilton shall continue to try to fill the gap of skilled employees by hiring "older workers."

HYATT CORPORATION

200 West Madison
Chicago, IL 60606
(312) 750-1234

Known for outstanding service, innovative style, and super-luxury hotels, Hyatt is owned by the Pritzker family of Chicago.

Hyatt Knows The Importance Of Seniors

Hyatt understands the importance of seniors in our aging marketplace. The hotel chain is currently looking to expand its senior programs, and continues to hire both full and part-time people at its many hotels and resorts. In 1989 Hyatt also opened an upscale retirement community called Classic Residence by Hyatt.

• •

MARRIOTT CORPORATION

10400 Fernwood Road
Bethesda, MD 20817
(301) 380-9000

The Marriott Corporation is one of the great entrepreneurial success stories of American business. Today, it is one of the leaders in the hospitality industry, employing over 200,000 people at its hotels, resorts, and retirement communities.

In addition to the Courtyard Inn and Fairfield Inn chains, Marriott provides food service management to large corporations and manages over 100 restaurants.

<u>Marriott Splits!</u>

In order to better pursue strategic growth, Marriott announced that it is separating into two companies:

1. **Marriott International** will manage Marriott's hotels
2. **Host Marriott Corporation** will own all real estate, airport, and highway concessions.

Marriott has an excellent reputation as a progressive employer. It has a corporate culture that places a strong emphasis on customer service, and these values should bring continued success.

• •

UNITED PARCEL SERVICE OF AMERICA, INC.

400 Perimeter Center
Atlanta, GA 30346
(404) 913-7123

Long known for its big brown delivery trucks, UPS has earned a solid reputation for its reliability in the growing parcel delivery industry.

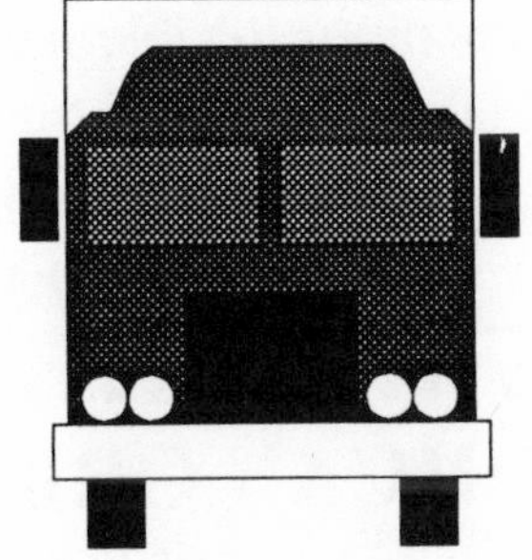

To compete head on with Federal Express and other major freight carriers UPS has invested heavily in new forms of technology in order to ship an estimated 3 billion packages and documents yearly.

UPS employs over 250,000 workers at offices and "hubs" throughout the country. Because of the tremendous surge in volume around the holidays, UPS has become an <u>excellent source for seasonal work at many of its distribution centers</u>, offering high wages and good benefits.

Working At or From Home

EMPLOYMENT OUTLOOK

More and more people are working at or from home for a wide variety of reasons: most simply can't find suitable employment in this harsh economy, some want to start a business of their own, and new advancements in technology are making "telecommuting" so much easier and attractive.

Nationwide, telecommuters (business or government employees who work at home instead of at the office) are growing faster in number than any other kind of home worker, and their numbers are increasing sharply every year. The integration of computers, telephones, and facsimile machines now allows home based workers to function as well, if not better, than those who are in the office full time. It also means companies can retain valuable employees and save money on overhead.

Working at or from home provides many work alternatives, especially for seniors: flexible schedules, better time management, the potential for earning full-time money in a part-time position, other ways to accommodate individual needs, less stress, ways to use skills and talents to start a business.

AMERICAN GREETINGS CORPORATION

10500 American Road
Cleveland, OH 44144
(216) 252-7300

Headquartered in Cleveland, Ohio, American Greetings is the 2nd largest producer of greeting cards (Hallmark is #1). It makes and sells greeting cards, wapping paper, stationery, calendars, gift items, and assorted accessories. Its licensing division offers such characters as Ziggy, the Care Bears, and Holly Hobbie.

Retirement is only ONE option!

With more than 20 offices and manufacturing facilities in the U.S. and given the continued rapid growth of the greeting card industry, American Greetings is a good place to consider working. It is always on the lookout for new talent and hires a great many freelance artists, writers, and photographers. Age is not a factor here, just "skill and dependability".

• •

AMERICAN RED CROSS

National Headquarters
17th & D Streets, N.W.
Washington, D.C. 20006
(202) 639-3146

Founded over a century ago, The American Red Cross has a mission as broad as it is important: to improve the quality of life, enhance self-reliance, and cope with emergencies.

Each year the Red Cross responds to disasters that occur around the world. It also offers extensive health and safety courses on everything from CPR and first aid to swimming and lifeguard training.

The Red Cross relies heavily on people of all ages and skill levels. Most of those who do work for this non-profit organization are volunteers, frequently working on flexible schedules. There are, however, a number of paid staff members. Minorities are definitely encouraged to apply. Recent openings called for a Product Manager for the American Red Cross Plasma Operation.

AMWAY CORPORATION

7575 E. Fulton Road
Ada, MI 49355
(616) 676-6000

The Original Multilevel Organization

Amway is one of the largest direct sales organizations in the world and considered by many to be the "original multilevel organization".

Amway sales representatives (distributors) earn commissions on their personal sales, as well as on the sales of distributors they have recruited.

Distributors sell everything from household and personal care products to nutritional supplements, educational books, furniture, and air purifiers.

Flexible Work Options

At Amway, people can work part-time or full-time, set their own hours, and plan their work schedule around their own particular lifestyle. No experience is needed. Training and support material are provided.

At Amway, "people can earn full-time pay for part-time hours".

• •

AVON PRODUCTS, INC.

9 West 57th Street
New York, NY 10019
(212) 546-6015

Avon is the world's largest direct seller and marketer of health and beauty products. Its 1.5 million Avon reps sell cosmetics, fragrances, toiletries, and a variety of gift items. Though its Giorgio Beverly Hills, Inc. unit, Avon sells prestigious retail fragrances such as Giorgio and Red.

<u>Largest Employer Of Women</u>

Avon is also the world's largest "employer" of women, although technically Avon sales reps are not actual employees, they are independent contractors.

<u>Avon offers extensive training, workshops, and opportunites for advancement</u>. A large percentage of women in management positions are full-time staff, and Avon has won numerous awards for advancement of women and minorities.

Avon continues to introduce new products, use 800 telephone numbers in advertising, explore retail opportunities, and considers increasing the number of its sales distribution centers. Like several other smart companies, Avon is using the "work-at-home" option as a means to attract top notch people.

• •

THE GALLUP ORGANIZATION, INC.

Suite 200
47 Hulfish Street
Princeton, NJ 08542
(609) 924-9600

The Gallup Organization is synonymous with modern market research. Gallup polls are cited with great regularity by newspapers worldwide. Large corporations routinely use Gallup to do marketing and attitude surveys.

Ideal For Retirees!

According to Kim Neighbor, a Field Administrator, Gallup is ideal for retirees. No experience is required. Door-to-door interviewing job opportunies are available in 360 sampling areas throughout the country, including Alaska and Hawaii.

Workers are considered independent contractors, work mostly on weekends(1-2 weekends per month), and are paid an hourly rate that differs depending upon the individual's experience and location.

"You need only be able to read well, talk with people, and have a dependable car." Those who'd like more information should contact:

The Gallup Organization, Inc.
Attention: Field Department
P.O. Box 310
Princeton, NJ 08542

●●

HALLMARK CARDS, INC.

2501 McGee
Kansas City, MO 64141
(816) 274-5111

Headquartered in Kansas City, Hallmark is the largest greeting card company in the U.S. and like its major competitor, American Greetings Company, is a highly regarded and very large employer of writers, artists, and photographers.

Turnover is dramatically lower with older workers!

Hallmark creates and sells greeting cards, wrapping paper, party supplies, crayons, ornaments, gift items, and assorted accessories. Hallmark products are sold in thousands of independently owned and company owned Hallmark Stores throughout the world.

Continued growth within the greeting card industry means Hallmark shall need a constant supply of "professionals" who can create and deliver high quality work.

• •

MARY KAY COSMETICS, INC.

8787 Stemmons Freeway
Dallas, TX 75247
(214) 630-8787

Mary Kay started this cosmetics empire on her kitchen table in 1963. Now there are over 2,000 employees and nearly 250,000 "beauty consultants" who invite customers to shows in their homes. Since they get paid a percentage of their sales rather than a salary, beauty consultants are considered independent contractors rather than employees.

Most beauty consultants work part-time. Virtually all of them are women.

Mary Kay's employees work in Dallas, or in distribution centers in Los Angeles, Atlanta, Chicago, and Piscataway, New Jersey. The beauty consultants who sell Mary Kay products work in every state in America and in 15 other countries.

U.S. OLYMPIC COMMITTEE

1750 East Boulder Street
Colorado Springs, CO 80909
(719) 578-4614

The Volunteer Program of the U.S. Olympic Committee is an excellent and very popular way to do some local community service
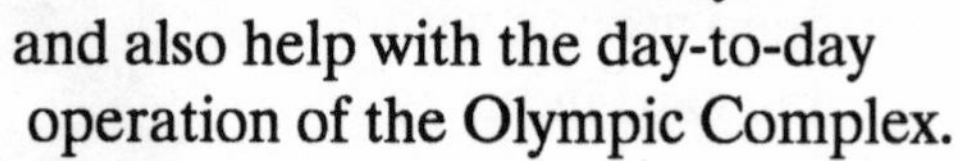
and also help with the day-to-day operation of the Olympic Complex.

According to Judith Bowers, Volunteer Coordinator, the majority of nearly 200 people who come into the program have an interest in sports.

"Volunteers help with mailings, file papers, do data entry. They also help with event management, sell tickets, and run the hospitality room".

Volunteers work out a schedule that's best for them, get discount tickets to sporting events at the Olympic Complex, and are even issued a meal ticket after so many hours of service. Best of all, says Judith Bowers, working here is an excellent way to meet lots of people from all over the country.

Index